No, We Can't

Sean,

Happy Father's Day!
May you always be that
"standing stone", a
testament of God's Working
in a life.

Love,
Mom

No, We Can't

Radical Islam, Militant Secularism
and the Myth of Coexistence

ROBERT STEARNS

Chosen
a division of Baker Publishing Group
Minneapolis, Minnesota

Published by Chosen Books
11400 Hampshire Avenue South
Bloomington, Minnesota 55438
www.chosenbooks.com

Chosen Books is a division of
Baker Publishing Group, Grand Rapids, Michigan

Printed in the United States of America

Library of Congress Cataloging-in-Publication Data
Stearns, Robert
    No, we can't: radical Islam, militant secularism, and the myth of coexistence/Robert Stearns
        p.   cm.
    Includes bibliographical references (p. 215).
    ISBN 978-0-8007-9520-7 (pbk. : alk. paper)
    1. Religions—Relations. 2. Coexistence. 3. International organization. 4. Religion and politics. 5. Radicalism—Religious aspects. 6. Religion and culture. I. Title.
BL410.S69 2011
297.2'83—dc23   2011026092

The Internet addresses, email addresses and phone numbers in this book are accurate at the time of publication. They are provided as a resource. Baker Publishing Group does not endorse them or vouch for their content or permanence.

In keeping with biblical principles of creation stewardship, Baker Publishing Group advocates the responsible use of our natural resources. As a member of the Green Press Initiative, our company uses recycled paper when possible. The text paper of this book is composed in part of post-consumer waste.

11   12   13   14   15   16   17   7   6   5   4   3   2   1

For Isaac, Daniel and Michael
in the hope you will inherit
a more genuinely tolerant world

Contents

Foreword

Several years ago, I was with my friend and mentor, Pastor Jack Hayford. We were walking and talking when he stopped abruptly. He laid his hand on my shoulder and looked me in the eye. "Robert," he said, "have you met Robert Stearns?" I told Pastor Jack that I had not. Pastor Jack looked me directly in the eye and said strongly, "Listen to me. You need to know Robert Stearns and his ministry."

It was all the encouragement I needed. Now, several years later, I have spoken at some of Eagles' Wings leadership gatherings, Robert has spoken here at one of our pastors' conferences at Gateway and we serve the Lord together in various ministry capacities.

Every once in a while, a book comes along that exactly captures the moment a generation is facing; it becomes a signpost that alters the direction of people's lives. A book can hit the bull's-eye center of the plans and purposes of God, inspiring those who read it to achieve their destinies. I believe the book you are holding in your hands is just such a book.

I have learned how important it is that we as the Body of Christ know how to apply the Word of God to each and every situation we encounter. The truth is that God's Word has everything to do with what is going on in global events today. The reason I am backing this book is because it is full of key insights that will empower you to put God's Word into action.

Like a modern-day prophet, Robert Stearns brings vital insight and strategy into how we can meet the challenges of our day. His integrity, character and commitment to the centrality of the Presence of God have caused Robert to be trusted and sought out by world leaders from every arena. He is brave enough to share a message that is not easy and comfortable and that will not be popular. It is nonetheless timely, perceptive and accurate, and we would do well to receive what it means for our lives so that we can live with conviction and purpose both now and in the days to come.

So, I'd like to look you directly in the eye and say to you, "Listen to me. Do you know Robert Stearns and his ministry? You need to."

Robert Morris, founding senior pastor, Gateway Church
(Dallas/Fort Worth Metroplex); host, *The Blessed Life*

Acknowledgments

This book would not have been possible without the extraordinary talent, anointing and commitment of Sarah Wolf. Though I provided the thought architecture for this work, she is the master wordsmith who built it from there. Her contribution is profoundly appreciated.

I also thank the following individuals for their invaluable assistance in completing this project: Aaron Derstine, Dr. Larry Keefauver, Ryan Mauro, Noa Bursie, David Danglis and Jane Campbell.

Introduction

"No, We Can't *What?*"

In 1981, Harvard-based business guru William Ury co-wrote a bestselling book on the strategies of negotiating. He called his book *Getting to Yes*. In it, he detailed all the constructive strategies that could be employed to help different parties overcome their obstacles and come to a place of agreement, even those parties who may long have been at odds with one another. The business world rejoiced, and more than five million copies of his affirmative message were sold.

In 2007, however, Ury released a new work. The title? Quite shockingly, *The Power of a Positive No*.

To explain what could be perceived as an about-face, Ury states that, in the years between the writing of the two books, he had come to some startling revelations. "All too often," he states, "we cannot bring ourselves to say *No* when we want to and know we should. . . . For even when agreements are reached, they are often unstable . . . because the real underlying issues have been avoided or smoothed over, *the problem only deferred*" (emphasis added).[1]

Over the years, I have come to some startling revelations on the topic of saying *no* myself. I used to be a "yes guy." I used to think that we all really were headed toward a place of agreement, of synthesis. And as often as I am tempted to think about how easy my life would be if I simply went back to this state of contented delirium, I cannot.

I still hope, I still believe, I still dialogue and I definitely still pray. Nothing brings me greater joy than to see harmony and true agreement between those who were formerly on opposite sides of the table. But in my twenty years of involvement with civic issues in America and discourse in the Middle East, I have come to the simple conclusion that, sometimes, no is the only honest, viable, positive answer one can give.

Titling a book is an interesting process. Words and phrases are examined, parsed and evaluated. When I first proposed this title for the book, it immediately raised some red flags. Did I want to send what could be perceived as a negative message? Did I want to risk coming across as divisive, discordant, close-minded? After all, no one was ever elected to political office by using "No, We Can't" as a campaign slogan! But gradually, the team working on the title came to believe that, indeed, someone needed to stand up and make this difficult, unpopular statement.

In the coming pages, we are not only going to discover precisely *why* we cannot do what many are claiming we can do, we are also going to discover what we truly *can* do to effect positive change in the world. I firmly believe there are countless people out there—good people, caring people, intelligent people, committed people—who sincerely desire to make a difference in the world, but whose efforts are stifled because they lack the one small key needed to unlock a giant door.

The world is shifting. The landscape of nations is changing—rapidly. Every morning I wake up and wonder what political revolution, border skirmish or socioeconomic catastrophe will have broken out overnight. The world is dissatisfied, baffled and craving transformation. Its search for answers has it roiling with ardor, animosity and zeal. Conversely, some who see no hope for transcendence are finding themselves mired in apathy and even despair—dedicating their lives to discrediting any trace of conviction, passion and faith others may hold.

It is against this backdrop that we emerge as those willing to search for and accept the true answers—even if they are not the warm, fuzzy ones we wished for. The temptation to pull the covers over our heads and go back to sleep remains enticing. I cannot help but recall the exchange that takes place between Frodo and Gandalf in the film adaptation of J. R. R. Tolkien's *Lord of the Rings*. After discovering that his life is about to get more difficult and uncomfortable than he ever could have imagined, the young protagonist petitions the wise, old counselor to see if there is any way out.

> *Frodo:* I wish none of this had happened.
> *Gandalf:* So do all who live to see such times. But that is not for them to decide. All we have to decide is what to do with the time that is given to us.[2]

Like this small, lone mortal who is put in the position of navigating a perilous world, we too have a choice:

> Do we want to deny reality, or face it?
> Do we want to pretend, or get real?
> Will we have the courage to say *no*, so that we can be empowered to say *yes*?

This a very exciting and liberating place to be. Who would want to live inside a fake, superficial and ultimately unsustainable myth when we can begin to flourish in a genuine, secure, ceaseless reality? Once you reject the false, you can embrace the true. If you allow yourself to say no, you can learn how to say yes. And the best part is that we are being given the chance to say yes to something that has the power not only to change *our* lives, but to change the world as well.

1

What the World Needs Now

There is a popular ad campaign I have often seen in large, international airports. One of the world's biggest banks—HSBC—launched its "different values" advertising campaign a few years ago, and by the way it has spread, I imagine it has brought them a lot of success. The message they communicate is a simple one: "Different values make the world a richer place." They suggest that people all over the world embrace a broad spectrum of ideas, and that no matter what you hope to accomplish in life, they're the ones to finance it. A perfectly logical assertion for a bank to make to potential customers. Sheer marketing brilliance.

Several times, walking down an immense corridor in a London or New York airport, I have looked up and seen these ads. Each ad consists of three gigantic posters that all repeat the exact same image. The only difference is that each poster bears a different word describing the image. One of these ads, for example, depicts three identical photos of the back of a person's shaved head. You can't tell if the person is male or female; the photograph is stark and neutral. Printed across the center of the first poster is the word *Style,* over the second poster *Soldier* and over the third *Survivor.* This illustrates, in a very concise and compelling way, how easy it is to have three different views of the exact same thing.

How about you? What word would you use to describe the many images you encounter? Have you taken a good, hard look at the world today?

By asking if you have looked at the world today, I'm merely pointing out the obvious fact that each of us *has* a view of the world, but few of us stop to contemplate it.

Shedding Some Light

If you got out of bed this morning, if you walked out your door, if you stood in line for a cappuccino or drove your car across town, you saw the world in a certain way while doing so. In fact, I would venture to say that the way you see the world is the very reason you got up this morning in the first place; that the way you see the world was your motive for leaving the house, your purpose for driving wherever it is you went. Rarely do we call into question the way we see the world—why we see it the way we do. Rarely do we question *why* we are thinking *what* we are thinking.

This book is my humble attempt to help change that. In the coming pages, I am inviting you to take a good, hard look with me at the world in which we live.

Jesus rebuked the religious cohorts of His day, saying,

> "When it is evening you say, 'It will be fair weather, for the sky is red'; and in the morning, 'It will be foul weather today, for the sky is red and threatening.' Hypocrites! You know how to discern the face of the sky, but you cannot discern the signs of the times."
>
> Matthew 16:2–3

Strong words! I, for one, don't want to fall into a religious mind-set that only operates within its own narrow frame of reference. The men Jesus addressed here were so adept at tracking something as mundane as the weather, but they were clueless about matters that carried dire consequences. Are we like that at times? Our radar is so acutely attuned to coughs coming from our children's bedrooms in the middle of the night, but we are often unable to discern how certain video games are desensitizing these same children to violence and cruelty.

Or perhaps the cares of this world have overwhelmed us to such a degree that we have grown too weary to challenge the ideas and practices that work overtime to uproot what we should be holding sacred. In all our busyness—taking the kids to soccer practice, balancing the checkbook, managing projects at the office and a thousand other important activities—have we forgotten *why* we are here in the first place? Have we forgotten about the hope we have within us to offer the rest of the world?

I don't want to be blind to what God is doing in my generation. I want to understand what is going on around me so that I can offer afresh to the world the eternal answer it is truly seeking. Followers of Jesus know deep in their hearts that He is Savior, Redeemer and the true Light of the World. We know there is a truth that transcends the circumstances we witness on a daily basis—dark and impossible as they may seem. Yet all too often, we have abdicated our position of responsibility and opted not to shine His light into the very darkness we are here to diminish.

Part of what it means to have an effective worldview is to take the time to actually *view the world* and what is happening in it. We need to intentionally bolster our understanding and alertness to how we can make a real and enduring difference in our world. And this is precisely what we are about to do.

Jesus said to those who followed Him, "You are the light of the world" (Matthew 5:14). Being acutely aware of the darkness that permeates the global landscape should not cause us to shrink back from living courageously. The presence of darkness should not weaken us, surprise us or intimidate us. Rather, it should propel us forward into our purpose as sons and daughters of the Light (see Ephesians 5:8). As we explore what is going on in the world around us and the role we have been given to play in it, we will be equipped to let our light shine to a world in desperate need.

The presence of darkness should not weaken us, surprise us or intimidate us.

Now that we have established that we all have a particular way of viewing the world, let us proceed to examine three specific value systems. Each one is led by a distinct mind-set. By identifying these three seminal worldviews, and by observing how they interact with one another, we will be better able to understand the place we have been called to occupy in the battle of life.

Three's Company

The HSBC people got it right when they so clearly presented us with three different views of the same thing. I am writing this book because, in the twenty years I have spent traveling, collaborating, preaching and serving throughout the nations, I have noticed the exact same trend. Whether looking at a photograph or looking at the world, I find that most people tend to see it in one of three distinct ways. There are, of course, countless points of view, and endless variations on the same theme, but there happen to be three primary worldviews that I encounter across the continents, generations and societies of our time. The more similarity that exists among individuals' worldviews, and the more these like-minded people unite together, the more powerful a force they become.

That said, I see three major players that have emerged from the stage of world history and are acting out the principal dramas of our present day. These are: a radicalized Islamic religious system; an aggressive, humanistic secularism; and a foundational biblical faith in the God of Israel. Most of the important events we hear about day to day could be traced back to one of these three superpowers.

When I describe these paradigms, I often find it helpful to refer to them as "houses." Houses are structures; and these structures are *houses of thought*. As in any house, these thought structures have entrances, exits, weight-bearing walls and sup- porting edifices. And perhaps more importantly, these thought structures, like physical houses, have people. What house would be complete without providing shelter for individuals, families and all those weary pilgrims who wander into the confines of its walls? Some people are born into a particular thought-house, and raised up to be products of their environment. Others move from one house to another because they are not satisfied with their view. These ideological structures are where thoughts pertain- ing to a specific worldview grow to fruition. They are also the foundational residences from which their respective systems of thought are subsequently lived out by those who believe them.

These ideological structures are where thoughts pertaining to a specific worldview grow to fruition.

Three schools of thought. Three global perspectives. Three cultural kingdoms. I often call them "The Three Houses." It may sound like a children's storybook, but I assure you, it does not read anything like one. Much of our conversation together will grapple with the nature of each house—how its influences shape and define—and what this translates into meaning for our everyday lives. The three primary ideological power structures responsible for fueling global affairs are:

- The house of Radical Islam
- The house of Militant Secularism
- The house of the Judeo-Christian worldview

Although we will, in a later chapter, examine the inner workings of each house in detail, I would like to briefly expand on them one by one.

The House of Radical Islam

Based on a committed devotion to the teachings of the Quran and the Prophet Muhammad, this ideology combines radicalized religious obedience to the god Allah with sociopolitical force, using many different tactics (including violence) to assert Muslim supremacy in the world. The ultimate goal of this house is to establish an Islamic caliphate, a ruling kingdom that holds all lands under its sway. Although "Radical Islam" is quickly becoming a household phrase in Western circles, just over a decade ago, it was largely unheard of.

> I am writing this book to provide believers with a strategic, up-to-date road map.

The House of Militant Secularism

Perhaps the least clearly defined house at first glance, Militant Secularism is nevertheless one of the most influential forces in the world today. Rooted in humanistic philosophy whose origins can be traced back to early Greek thought, this paradigm is all encompassing and deeply entrenched in prevailing cultures across the developed world. Its militancy is not usually a literal militancy. Rather, its aggression lies in its appeal to the independent, prideful human spirit and the power of human accomplishments. Its prevailing belief is that it is unlikely there is a god, and if there is, this "god" can be defined by us, because human beings determine their own destinies.

The House of the Judeo-Christian Worldview

Even though this house is my home, it is still by far the most difficult for me to define. Adhering to the basic moral code derived from the Ten Commandments and Jesus' teachings, this unique value system has grown to become the world's single largest religion. Its root system is very clear—springing out of the Old and New Testaments—but what is less clear is the actual expression of this worldview in what is commonly called the post-Christian West. Historically, the creeds of the faith have kept it strong and served as guardrails along the way. In recent times, cultural expressions labeled "Christian" but lacking real devotion and biblical truth have diluted the strength of the faith in this house.

Pretty sobering stuff.

I am writing this book to provide believers with a strategic, up-to-date road map that will help them navigate their life purpose. Broadly speaking, our purpose is to fully utilize the lives God has given us to glorify Him and inspire as many others as possible to embrace His Lordship. Too often, we Christians— who should be courageously serving, understanding and leading as representatives of the Kingdom of God—find ourselves marginalized and silenced in our quest. If we seek God, however, He will let us find Him (see Jeremiah 29:13). He will give us everything we need for life and godliness (see 2 Peter 1:3), everything we need to live effectively for Him.

I believe the first step in that process involves Him giving us an understanding—indeed, *His* understanding—of our world.

The View

Does the term *worldview* still sound theoretical to you? Abstract? Inconsequential? Cerebral? Does it sound like a mere concept that only exists in undergraduate sociology textbooks? I assure you, it is anything but. In fact, there is no action, thought or desire we have ever had that has not had a worldview attached to it.

You are living inside a worldview right now. (Your own.) Wherever you are sitting, standing, leaning or reclining, you are, right now, viewing the world from a certain vantage point that is uniquely yours. And I am not referring to what objects you can or cannot see within the rest of the space. I am referring to the fact that the reaction you had when you saw the cover of this book might have been completely different from the reaction the nearest person to you had when he or she first saw it.

> There is no action, thought or desire we have ever had that has not had a worldview attached to it.

This difference, in and of itself, would not serve as a significant cause of conflict in our world today. I'm sure you've never come to blows with other shoppers because you liked a book cover they didn't. It is ridiculous even to imagine such a thing! Yet it illustrates an important point. Because we are so immersed in our own ways of thinking, we often forget that other worldviews exist, and that they are closer to colliding with our own than we may realize.

You Are Here

Picture a giant world map sprawled across the length of a wall. The most prominent feature of the map is the myriad different nations scattered across the continents. These multicolored, jagged-edged shapes make the earth's surface look like a haphazard checkerboard. Some nations are enormous; some are small; some are touching the sea; some are landlocked. A few nations are so tiny the names they bear have to be strategically placed elsewhere so that the words do not completely cover up the minute slivers of landmass.

With few exceptions, national borders are long-established, plainly marked, uncontested territories. There is even a common system in place to allow travel from one nation to another. If you are a Canadian who wants to tour the vineyards of Italy, you simply obtain a passport and the proper visa, if required. You then travel to the country, go through customs, receive a stamp on your passport, and you are off on your Italian adventure. It sounds easy, safe and totally risk-free. So, what's the problem?

The issue lies in the fact that the national borders that clutter our map do not mean what they did in the past. One can no longer take for granted that the people one encounters in Italy will speak Italian, think Italian or even *be* Italian in any historic sense of the term. No, our world today cannot be categorized into cleanly divided, shaded boxes that relate to one another in predictable ways. The boundary lines are being erased, and other lines of division are emerging in which geography is not the main factor.

These worldviews (or "houses") are rapidly becoming the new scaffolding upon which the sociopolitical world is built.

Naturally, groups of people who think alike will always tend to remain or gravitate together—resulting in physical regions being colored in a particular light. The cultural forces we are talking about are by no means tied down in limited areas of influence. The fault lines that naturally exist between those of opposing worldviews run through national borders as if they're not even there. They obscure ethnic groups, divide families, separate friends. Now that the world is flat, these worldviews (or "houses") are rapidly becoming the new scaffolding upon which the sociopolitical world is built.

Really Different Values

Let's think back to the international ad campaign I described at the start of this chapter. You may even have come across one of HSBC's "different values" ad series yourself while traveling or while leafing through a magazine in the doctor's office. If we are going to have an honest discussion of what it means to have different values, we need to acknowledge that the values illustrated in the particular ad I mentioned appeal to universal themes that are not divisive in nature. For instance, you may have a clean-shaven friend whom you feel looks sophisticated. You may also know of at least one young man you admire who has his head shaved because he is part of the armed forces. And, you may even have a friend who lost her hair while undergoing chemotherapy treatments. The different values the ad is conjuring up are all fairly easy to identify with and understand.

> While 9/11 was a literal collision between planes and buildings, it represented the collision of intangible forces even more monumental.

I cannot help but wonder what would happen if one of the ads featured a series depicting Manhattan's Twin Towers disintegrating in smoke and flames on September 11, 2001. Over the first poster, the word *Terror,* the second *Victory,* the third *Justice.* No doubt this would strike a deeper chord within passersby. The reason it would is because the sentiments being expressed represent opposing views held by vast numbers of people. While 9/11 was a literal collision between planes and buildings, it represented the collision of intangible forces even more monumental: worldviews in opposition to one another.

For Christians, we know it is entirely possible for two people to be living on the same street, yet existing in two entirely separate kingdoms. Everyone sets up camp in a particular kingdom here on earth, wherever that may be. You may have experienced this by going over to the house of a friend who is serving a "false god." The minute you step foot on his terrain, you are standing in another kingdom. The atmosphere within his home will bear the characteristics of that kingdom. Depending on what belief system is in place, you may find yourself feeling depressed, bewildered, enticed or apathetic. These feelings, if succumbed to, can go so far as to manifest in tangible ways, leaving you exhausted, argumentative, frightened or even sick to your stomach. By being properly trained, however, as emissaries for the Kingdom of God, not only can we withstand the onslaught of evil, we can bring a blessing that reverses the curse in our friend's life. This is what we're here to do!

We are the light of the world, the salt of the earth. We are to diffuse the fragrance of the knowledge of God wherever we go (see 2 Corinthians 2:14). As we can readily see each time we turn on the six o'clock news, there is no end of mayhem, disaster and heartbreak in this world. We need to begin exercising our spiritual senses and operating in discernment as we look at the world around us. It is a spiritual battle we are called to win. To achieve success, we must allow the Holy Spirit full and complete access to our own hearts, minds and bodies. Once He is enthroned in our souls, our homes, our churches, our communities, we then have a chance to influence the lives of others.

> For though we walk in the flesh, we do not war according to the flesh. For the weapons of our warfare are not carnal but mighty in God for pulling down strongholds, casting down arguments and every high thing that exalts itself against the knowledge of God, bringing every thought into captivity to the obedience of Christ.
>
> 2 Corinthians 10:3–5

Admitting We Have a Problem

I contemplated opening this book with, "Hello, my name is Robert, and I'm an optimist." I have yet to find a twelve-step program designed to meet the needs of me and my fellow idealists, but true to my nature, I still haven't given up hope there's one out there.

I am an optimist—really, I am. I am a glass-half-full kind of guy. My nature and personality are such that I am continually looking for ways to "make things work" between people. I am a bridge-builder, a friend-maker, a peace-seeker.

Just because I'm discussing extremely volatile and contentious divisions that exist in our world today, please do not assume I'm satisfied with the status quo. I assure you, I take no pleasure that our beloved little planet seems about ready to explode from strife and discord. I would like nothing better than to wake up one day and discover that I have been wrong all along: that the radical Islamists no longer want to kill me; that the militant secularists are no longer intent on turning my Christmas tree into a "holiday shrub." But I am beginning to come to terms with the fact that hell is more likely to freeze over than for either of those things to happen. I would like nothing better than to be wrong, but I fear on this one that I am, unfortunately, very right.

As we will go into in later chapters, it is indeed possible for those with divergent beliefs to live peaceably side by side. But to do so they must agree to abide by a certain set of rules, which they must acknowledge are supreme and exclusive. If these rules permit people the right to hold their own opinions and ideas, everything will go smoothly. It is when the rules are altered beyond recognition that the game can no longer be played.

In his 1945 allegorical novella *The Great Divorce*, C. S. Lewis follows several characters on a fantastical bus journey through the afterlife, examining the choices they make that lead them to their final destinations. In the preface to this fictional journey, Lewis tells us:

Blake wrote the Marriage of Heaven and Hell. . . . The attempt [to make that marriage] is based on the belief that reality never presents us with an absolutely unavoidable "either-or"; that, granted skill and patience and (above all) time enough, some way of embracing both alternatives can always be found. . . . This belief I take to be a disastrous error. We are not living in a world where all roads are radii of a circle and where all, if followed long enough, will therefore draw gradually nearer and finally meet at the centre: rather in a world where every road, after a few miles, forks into two, and each of those into two again, and at each fork you must make a decision. Even on the biological level life is not like a river, but like a tree. It does not move toward unity but away from it.[1]

If Lewis is right in believing that people cannot, in and of themselves, achieve lasting peace and unity, then the global turmoil that has been erupting all around us may be only the initial tremors of a seismic shift, the likes of which we have never seen. And if that is what we're in for, we as believers need to be equipped in our prayers, our worship, our lifestyles and our witness as never before. We will take an in-depth look at simple, everyday tactics that you and I can use to activate our faith in God and in His Kingdom. If there ever were a time when we must let our light shine in the darkness, it is now.

Are you open to joining me on this journey? I am not offering you "nine easy steps to a stress-free Christmas" or "four ways to be liked by everyone at church." If you are looking for someone to tell you how to have a nice, easy, comfortable life, there are plenty of books out there that will do just that. This is not one of them. This is a book for those who want to be awakened, who want to have their priorities challenged and comfort zones stretched, who want to live a life worthy of the calling they have received (see Ephesians 4:1).

We need to become forces for change wherever God has placed us. I guarantee you that, if you embark with me down this road, you will be equipped with cutting-edge understanding of what is going on around you and how you can effectively live out a biblical worldview in the midst of it. I want us to discover how our lives can count eternally by the way we live them today.

31

I believe God is offering us the opportunity to be His ambassadors, His artisans, His educators, His messengers so that the one true and living God is made known in an undeniable way. You and I have been uniquely selected to be alive at this strategic hour in human history. Lives hang in the balance. Whole people groups hang in the balance. There are "multitudes, multitudes in the valley of decision" (Joel 3:14). They are actively seeking a voice to guide them toward the only thing that will ultimately satisfy their souls. They are listening for a voice. Will they hear yours?

> **We need to become forces for change wherever God has placed us.**

2

The End of the World As We Know It

Before we get to the meat of this book, there is one more course I would like to serve up; I believe it will enhance everything else to come. Prior to studying the complex interplay of world civilizations, I would like us to take a step back to take in the big picture. If you will allow me to pause here for a moment, we will gain some important context for what we are about to learn; namely, the point in world history at which these events are taking place.

The End

This is not a book about the end of the world. Well, it is not supposed to be, at least.

What I started out to do was to write a book about the current state of global affairs—to shed light on the epic events we see unfolding around us daily. And, chapter by chapter, you will find that this is indeed what I have done. We will canvass continents, epochs and daytime TV, gaining key insights along the way that will help us make sense of the growingly complex world in which we live.

The irony lies in the fact that, at this moment in time, the events unfolding around us every day and the events one would typically think of as marking the end of the world are becoming increasingly difficult to distinguish from one another. In other words, writing a book about current affairs these days is all but synonymous with writing a book about the climax of human civilization.

> The events unfolding around us every day and the events one would typically think of as marking the end of the world are becoming increasingly difficult to distinguish.

Now, let me assert that not only do we not know when the "end of the world" is going to take place, but we do not even know precisely what it will entail. Am I referring to the classic "fire and brimstone" scenario? Possibly. We can do our best to understand what is to come, but there will always be at least some element of speculation in even the most learned scholar's predictions. The undeniable fact, however, is that thinking people everywhere, from disparate walks of life, agree on one thing: There are major, unprecedented forces at work right now that seem to be, of their own volition, moving us toward some manner of cataclysmic shift. Whatever name people give it, the end of all that we have ever known is nearer than it has ever been.

Just how near is "near" is a matter open for interpretation. But unlike in times past, when it was just a few lone voices claiming a far-fetched creed that doomsday was upon us, today there are numerous belief systems—whether overtly religious, sociological, ecological or otherwise scientific—lining up in agreement that the end is (very) near.

Apocalypse Makes Strange Bedfellows

A short time ago, I was on a domestic flight reading a Christian book that held the "2012 phenomenon" up to the light of biblical prophecy. Sitting in the seat beside me was a normal-looking, middle-aged woman who asked what I thought of the book I was reading. She went on to tell me she had read it herself; she had read everything on the topic she could get her hands on. I assumed she was a fellow believer in Jesus, but as she explained to me her beliefs about the end times, I saw this was not quite the case.

This kindly woman, who was knitting a sweater for her new-born baby granddaughter, went on to matter-of-factly explain to me that we were living at the end of the last cycle of the ancient Mayan calendar—to conclude on 12/21/2012. At this point, she said, all of us, who throughout our reincarnated lifetimes have learned to become good people, would undergo a collective shift in consciousness. We would then spiritually evolve into four-dimensional beings that would be transported to another planet to live a harmonious, celestial existence. This very sincere woman was a medium from a New Age spiritist community who believed it was her mission to help people cross from one life into the next.

Needless to say, it was a memorable experience. It was also revelatory for me in that it showed so clearly how someone with beliefs extremely contradictory to my own was contemplating the same questions I was about the tenor of our times.

Consider these additional illustrations from three divergent faith groups:

- Of the many biblical prophecies fulfilled in modern times, the reestablishment of the State of Israel has perhaps received the most attention. The turmoil surrounding this tiny nation is something that most people on the planet are acutely aware of. The book of Ezekiel foretells an invasion of Israel by surrounding nations and an ensuing battle, which precedes the worldwide battle of Armageddon (see chapters 38–39). Today, Israel makes the headlines on a daily basis due to the contention it faces from surrounding nations, which openly declare their commitment to Israel's destruction, just as Scripture foretells. With a madman dictator at the helm of a nuclear Iran, the world is holding its breath, wondering not *if*, but *when* the epic attack against Israel will begin.

> **Israel makes the headlines on a daily basis due to the contention it faces.**

- Numerous Mid-East experts and political analysts are worried that the politics of Iranian President Mahmoud Ahmadinejad are being fueled by an eschatological Shia belief that a violent war needs to precede the return of the twelfth Imam. This long-awaited religious leader will usher in the end of the current age and bring the entire human population under Islamic rule. The fear is that Ahmadinejad will recklessly use the nuclear arms Iran is developing to trigger a colossal war that could be described as nothing short of apocalyptic. In the meantime, he appears to be readying the Islamic Republic to receive its Mahdi (or Savior) by devoting millions of dollars to an elaborate mosque and educating devout Muslims about the apocalyptic role they play in this end-time scenario.

- The incredibly young Baha'i faith has grown at an unprecedented rate, and has become a major player on the religious scene since its inception in the mid-nineteenth century. It is growing in popularity within humanist societies (not normally considered religious) because of its ecumenical nature. Baha'i followers are devoted to establishing a new world order. They are working diligently to achieve a one-world government and one world religion. It is their stated purpose to usher in a global leader who will bring about world peace, which happens to fit the age-old description of the Antichrist. And considering the staggering amount of influence the Baha'is hold within the UN, they do not seem to be very far from achieving their goal.

These examples, from diverse religious expressions, make a compelling point. But concluding that those who hold to no faith at all are free from end-time anxieties could not be less true. On the contrary, atheists and those who believe the earth is our final destination seem to be panicking more than anyone else.

Secularists Concur

Yale-trained historian and economist Neil Howe co-authored a series of bestselling books based on extensive study of American history. In their widely respected seminal work, *The Fourth Turning,* Howe and his co-writer, William Straus, explore unmistakable sociological patterns that repeat themselves cyclically, in which values shift and new public mores are established. They identify four seasons that progress from a "high," to an "awakening," to an "unraveling" and, finally, to a "crisis." Citing

> Atheists and those who believe the earth is our final destination seem to be panicking more than anyone else.

the present day as an era marked by corruption, irresponsibility, dissonance and despair, these secular prophets propose America is undergoing a season of unraveling and entering into *the fourth turning*—a period of extraordinary calamity. Like past nationwide peril, which has included wars and famines, this dark season of collective metamorphosis will shake any degree of stability we have been able to cling to. But unlike past crises, many view the impending one as more hazardous, threatening and, perhaps, even final.

Such bleak forecasts can give way to despondency and lead people to give themselves over to hedonism. But on the opposite extreme, many who have no hope but in this world understandably end up trying to save it—becoming avid in their efforts and hostile toward anyone who won't join them. There is a growing number of people who are hyper-concerned over the destruction of the environment and what they predict will be the inevitable result that follows: the termination of our species.

> The decaying state of our physical world agrees with Bible prophecies that warn of great ecological distress slated for the last days.

While those of us who do believe in the coming of Messiah have a very different view of such issues than environmentalists have, there are real issues that have a real impact. Because we will all, for better or worse, be living on the same planet until whatever is going to happen actually *does*, it makes no sense to disregard the deteriorating condition of Planet Earth. The sad state in which we find ourselves stems from the fallen nature of human beings and the devastation they have inflicted on the rest of creation. As with the views of other faiths that are in total opposition to one another yet share a remarkably compatible timeline for the end of the world, the decaying state of our physical world agrees with Bible prophecies that warn of great ecological distress slated for the last days.

> I looked when He opened the sixth seal, and behold, there was a great earthquake; and the sun became black as sackcloth of hair, and the moon became like blood. And the stars of heaven fell to

the earth, as a fig tree drops its late figs when it is shaken by a mighty wind. Then the sky receded as a scroll when it is rolled up, and every mountain and island was moved out of its place.

Revelation 6:12–14

No longer are passages like these taken merely figuratively. Many feel the prophecies that portray the sun turning into darkness and the moon into blood could be accurate descriptions of a time when sunlight is blocked from the earth's atmosphere due to natural or man-made disasters.

This could happen through any number of causes. For instance, there are seven known supervolcanoes located underneath the earth's crust. These enormous, highly volatile, dormant pockets of lava are considered to be among the most powerful forces on the planet and are poised to wreak havoc markedly greater than even the worst eruptions from ordinary volcanoes. Not only would the explosion of a supervolcano be lethal enough to snuff out life on an entire continent, but the resulting volcanic winter caused by the enormous amount of ash in the atmosphere could disrupt the food supply and result in global famine.

Unfortunately, this is not merely idle doomsday speculation. A series of volcanic disturbances on disparate islands, capped off by the largest volcanic eruption in over a thousand years, brought about massive climate imbalance in April 1815. It was then that Indonesia's Mount Tambora erupted, resulting in the eventual deaths of over 100,000 people.[1] It also triggered a tsunami, worldwide crop failures, large-scale famine and disease and "the year without a summer."[2] In light of this, it is reasonable that many in North America are nervous about the colossal mass of molten lava that sits beneath Yellowstone National Park, which scientists warn is long overdue for another eruption, and is, year by year, pushing its way closer to the surface.

The very real possibility of nuclear war looms over us as well. Not only are there nation-states poised to wage atomic warfare against one another, there are tens of thousands of rogue nuclear warheads that could be launched from any number of locations by terrorist infrastructures. Aside from the staggering amount of life that would be lost initially, these attacks could cause a "nuclear winter," which, like a volcanic winter, would block the sun's rays over vast areas of the earth's surface for up to several years (depending on the number and size of the bombs).

Even without large-scale catastrophes such as these, we seem to be doing a pretty good job of destroying the planet ourselves, one day at a time.

Going, Going . . . Green?

Welcome to what many are calling the Environmental Age. It is not as picturesque as it may sound. The term comes from the overwhelming number of critical issues we are facing as members of earth's biosphere. In case you don't have enough to worry about already, here are some life-threatening concerns to think over the next time you are stuck in traffic: ozone depletion, toxic waste, soil erosion, smog, deforestation, light pollution, urban sprawl, acid rain, nuclear meltdowns, overgrazing, soil contamination, ocean acidification, slash-and-burn agriculture, destruction of biodiversity, groundwater pollution, energy shortage, depletion of fossil fuels, chlorofluorocarbons, electromagnetic radiation, genetically modified food organisms, habitat destruction, carbon emissions, overfishing, medical waste and species extinction—to name a few.

Many specialists in the field agree that the human race cannot go on living the way it currently does for longer than a few more decades. They predict that if human beings are to survive, they will do so only in population pockets scattered around the globe, barely surviving in what would be a new Dark Age.

40

Certain evangelicals are quick to dismiss these concerns, citing that these future conjectures are not compatible with biblical eschatology. There are, however, some important things that believers can both glean from and contribute to the environmental conversation. I would contend that we are the best motivated to understand and respond. Who should care more about the conservation of our resources than the ones who believe it is their job to wisely steward them? It seems to me that those who believe they know the One who created the world should care a great deal about preserving His handiwork from annihilation—not for its own sake, but for the sake of the Creator.

And, if it's just alarm we're looking for, there are, unfortunately, more than enough ecological dynamics negatively affecting our everyday lives that are uncontestable. The evidence is so apparent we couldn't ignore it if we tried. If all this isn't distressing enough for you, there is yet another major crisis brewing that is even more central to our existence: the earth's water supply.

Building Blocks Crumbling

Did you know that experts are predicting the world could conceivably go to war over water within the next fifty years?[3] The battle lines are being drawn as water—the most essential building block of all living things—becomes a hot-topic commodity with commercial and political ramifications. The United States is already reprioritizing its foreign policy around water, which has replaced oil as the most valuable resource on the planet.[4] In addition to ecological deprivation caused by natural disasters, water scarcity is being brought on by enormous, multinational corporations that are moving into developing countries and small town America alike, robbing economically vulnerable communities of their water sources to make a profit.

This is an extremely critical issue that is not going away. As it becomes more and more difficult for groundwater to be replenished and for watersheds to sustain themselves, the situation becomes increasingly desperate. Water tycoons move in and literally buy up this vital resource, exploiting it in the same way the earth's oil has been exploited—one story of corruption we are all too familiar with. But as the geopolitical web becomes ever more tense and charged, things will go from bad to worse, and the question we will have to face is this: Who controls the world's drinking water, and how much are they going to charge us for this essential life-sustaining resource?

> Most thinking people would agree on at least one thing: We're all in the same boat. And it's sinking.

Sadly, the condition of the global food supply isn't looking any better. Not only are there more than nine hundred million people estimated to be undernourished today,[5] the situation could worsen dramatically in years to come. The tragic reason for this, however, does not lie in food production; it lies in food accessibility. It is not that various geographic areas aren't inherently capable of growing the food needed to sustain their populations; they are. It's that the convoluted nature of the global economy we find ourselves in has caused whole areas that were once self-sufficient to become food-dependent. With international water and food supplies in extremely fragile condition, the very building blocks of our lives are tottering precariously on the edge of a once-stable existence.

From the search for the twelfth Imam to the priorities of the New Age to evangelical Christian conviction to the Greenpeace agenda (and just about everything in between), whatever commonality we lack in our worldviews, most thinking people would agree on at least one thing: We're all in the same boat. And it's sinking.

Three—Two—One

I would like to leave us with the thoughts of three prominent, well-known leaders who each represent one of the areas of global influence this book is dedicated to examining: Radical Islam, Militant Secularism and the Judeo-Christian worldview. These leaders are reflecting and shaping the mind-set of millions of people. They also have the influence and power base to move cultural leaders to action. Remarkably, these three fundamentally differing voices, representing fundamentally differing viewpoints, all agree that the world as we know it is on the brink of demise.

Radical Islam

Many Westerners are understandably perplexed by the ranting of Iranian President Mahmoud Ahmadinejad. This is because his grandiose vitriol can only be properly understood in light of its true intent. His infamous speech to the United Nations General Assembly, for instance, actually contained an underlying warning to the world—a declaration of the inevitability of global Islamic dominance. It was also a call to action for the Shiite religious community to initiate an end-time war on all who resist their eschatological agenda.

> Today, we should define our economic, cultural and political policies based on the policy of Imam Mahdi's return.
>
> —Iranian President Mahmoud Ahmadinejad[6]

Militant Secularism

Prominent politician and environmental activist Al Gore has expressed his belief that, if we do not make significant strides in saving our planet within the next ten years, it may be too late to avoid irreparable damage.

> Global warming is a strategic threat. The concentration of carbon dioxide and other heat-absorbing molecules has increased by almost 25 percent since World War II, posing a worldwide threat to the earth's ability to regulate the amount of heat from the sun retained in the atmosphere.[7]

We know from the history of climate changes that they can cause unprecedented social and political upheavals.[8]

—Former vice president
and environmental activist Al Gore

Judeo-Christian Worldview

In his book *Can America Survive?*, *New York Times* bestselling author John Hagee cites ten scriptural reasons why "we are the terminal generation."

It is a perfect storm that has been brewing for centuries that is about to explode in all its fury affecting the lives of every person on planet Earth.

—Pastor John Hagee[9]

Whatever your personal convictions are about the status of the world today, it ought to arrest the attention of all of us that these three examples (and many others) point in a surprisingly similar and foreboding direction. Each comment reflects the core belief of millions of people and provides a common thread—the end of the world as we know it. In the minds of many people groups on earth is the recurring nightmare of an impending apocalypse.

Apocalypse Prime Time

With all this doom and gloom, it's no wonder people mentally check out and do everything they can to avoid thinking about it. The entertainment industry—that multi-billion-dollar machine that never stops its glowing, pulsating, mind-numbing pull on the human soul—is one of the single most powerful man-made forces operating on the earth today. Because of it, we live in a perpetual state of distraction—connected to a cyber reality, but not to actual reality.

Consider this: According to Nielsen ratings as of 2009, the *average* American watches approximately 34 hours of television each week, not including video, online or other forms of electronic entertainment.[10] In addition, 65 percent of U.S. households also play video games, and the average "gamer" spends eighteen hours a week playing them.[11] Moviemaking continues as a massive entertainment industry, surpassing $10 billion in ticket sales in the United States alone in both 2009 and 2010.[12]

The stuff of 1950s sci-fi movies—overgrown gorillas, giant ants, menacing squids, random aliens and, of course, *The Blob*—sounds like bedtime stories to us today. Even if films like *The Incredible Shrinking Man* and *Creature from the Black Lagoon* were genuinely frightening to people back then, they were made up of far-off, fictional scenarios that were far from being technologically or biologically possible. You can imagine a 1950s parent rushing into a child's bedroom to calm her down after she has had a film-induced nightmare, saying, "No, honey, there are no such things as giant ants. . . . Go back to sleep." What is more difficult to imagine is a parent trying to soothe a frightened child who has watched a sci-fi movie from our era.

"No, honey, there is no such thing as bioterrorism. . . ."

"No, honey, no one could clone your DNA and replace you. . . ."

"No, honey, a man-made particle accelerator in Switzerland is not going to explode and blow up the entire planet. . . ."

There is so little imagination required to make a horror film these days! All producers need to do is watch the six o'clock news to learn how the latest technological developments could be used against us, and they have their plot. There is virtually no difference between the summer blockbusters we see the public flocking to and the imminent realities we have to deal with.

45

The ironic truth is that, in the 21st century, the nightmare is more comforting than the facts awaiting us when we wake up. A film depicting the battle of Armageddon is less threatening than a literal end-time clash of civilizations. Perhaps this is why Columbia Pictures' 2009 action film entitled *2012* is reported to have grossed over $769 million worldwide.[13] If we have such real anxieties about the end of life on earth, why would we want to create imaginary scenarios depicting our worst fears? Because the film, at least, you can turn off. Have we created these apocalyptic amusements as a way of making ourselves feel more in control of our lives? Whatever the case, it is the unquestionable truth that our obsession with the end of the world is blinding us to the end of the world.

> Our obsession with the end of the world is blinding us to the end of the world.

Even Hollywood is in agreement that it is "the end of the world as we know it," or, "TEOTWAWKI," which you may have noticed being used in social media and other contexts. No one in the film industry or anywhere else is imagining a bright, happy world of tomorrow. Everyone knows the future is scary, and they know this because *the future is now.* In fact, the only conjectures Hollywood can come up with for mankind's continued existence could all be lumped into one genre: post-Apocalyptic, which is quite possibly the only thing scarier than an apocalypse now.

The Sky Is Falling

Even if you're one to chalk up all these conjectures to mere hearsay; even if it sounds to you like the cartoon character Chicken Little running around, hysterically shouting, "The sky is falling!," I hope we can agree on one, inarguable point: No matter what may or may not happen tomorrow, the cataclysmic events of today are more than enough to drastically upset the balance of life on the planet. And in a world turned upside down, the sky is already under our feet.

Indeed, it is not just the over-90s demographic that finds the state of the world appalling. Baby boomers, Gen Xers, and even the Millennial Generation—still so young they are only now coming to think critically about the world around them—all seem to reach the same consensus: "This world is a crazy place, and if it is not going to spin completely out of control, something has got to be done."

Again, just what needs to be done in order to stabilize our world and set it back on its proper axis will vary as much as the individual to whom you ask the question. Assuming it is even possible to "turn the world right side up" at this point, what would it look like to do so? What is the norm we would try to get back to? What would a healthy, stable, functional world look like? Are there certain fundamental characteristics that an idyllic culture should include? I believe there are. Out of the myriad of cultural expressions that have existed from the dawn of time, let us take a look at what makes for a healthy culture. We will then be better equipped to assess each of the three cultural houses.

3

Cultural Kingdoms

When we stop to think about why we do the things we do, we begin to understand what culture is. Why do you stop at a stop sign—or get that sense of dread when flashing lights in your rearview mirror remind you that you didn't? Why do you sip a tiny cup of grape juice at a Sunday morning church service, or indulge in a hearty slice of pumpkin pie on the fourth Thursday of every November?

Is the fact that we live in a specific culture—that we most likely pass daily through several subcultures—even on our radar? Are we aware of the culture that we shape, and that shapes us? Culture is the backdrop against which our lives take place. In this life, nothing ever just "happens." Rather, there is a context, a cause and a structure for everything we experience. Among other things, culture is made up of stories, holidays, prayers, language, behaviors and a core moral code. Even if you decide that you do not want to live according to any of the above, you have already made a value decision on the type of culture you *do* want to live in. But few of us are that independent. We allow the environment and the people around us to shape us into the type of people we become.

Remember our three houses?

- The house of Radical Islam
- The house of Militant Secularism
- The house of the Judeo-Christian worldview

They did not just suddenly appear on the scene. Each is a cultural kingdom that has evolved and unfolded historically within the context of various people groups. Their beliefs, practices and rituals make sense to each house even if the other houses cannot fathom them. People within each house cannot imagine living anywhere else, thinking any other way or doing life differently. Let me explain.

Where Do We Live?

There was an amusing commercial you may remember seeing on TV not long ago. It advertised a nationwide chain of drugstores, suggesting to viewers that those stores were the best places to run to at the last minute for items you forgot to buy, or if something unfortunate happened and you needed a particular product to fix the situation. The commercial seemed to make a vivid impression on people.

> Culture is the backdrop against which our lives take place.

The ad began with a series of aerial shots overlooking idyllic landscapes—a quiet marine harbor, rolling green hills, beautifully decorated homes and nostalgic images of Main Street, U.S.A. There was tranquil instrumental music playing in the background, while a voice-over began to describe this town— a place called "Perfect, U.S.A."—in which nothing ever went wrong. There was never a stain on the carpet, a shortage of cash, printing errors or seasonal allergies. No such problems existed in "Perfect." The commercial concluded with the narrator stating, "Of course, we don't live anywhere near 'Perfect,' so there's *Walgreens*—with everything needed for the real world."

All of us can relate to this scenario because so many things go wrong for us in any given day: the kids miss the bus, a water main breaks, we misplace our car keys, we run out of milk. After watching this commercial, though, I never found myself thinking about the necessity of a 24-hour corner drugstore, but of "Perfect, U.S.A.," the fictional setting where nothing ever goes wrong. I know it sounds odd, but this flawless, imaginary world intrigued me.

What would a perfect world be like?

I am not advocating for a utopian experiment; I do not expect there to be peace on earth until God Himself brings it. Rather, contemplating "Perfect, U.S.A." led me to wonder just how far I actually *do* live from "Perfect."

Perfection may be unattainable, but what would an *ideal* world look like? And for that matter, of the many social orders currently at work in the world, are some better than others? Are there objective criteria that could serve to determine what should pass for reality? These are the questions we need to ask ourselves if we are to have a serious conversation about cultural worldviews.

Ideal, U.S.A.

Is it possible to take the temperature of a culture? Is it possible to tell if it is sick or healthy? If cultures are entities that can be measured, they can also be compared. Is it fair to say that one culture is better than another? Are there enduring values to which all cultures should aspire? And if so, what are they? If we are to answer questions about how culture affects our lives, we must make sure we have a clear understanding of what culture is.

So what is *culture*? The word itself is Latinate and can be traced back to the word *colere,* which means "to cultivate." The definition implies a process whereby certain characteristics are brought to a fuller and more perfect form through intentional study or development. Because of this, the word is often used to describe excellence in the arts. You may have heard someone say of a leading academic or musician, "She is a very cultured person."

Are there enduring values to which all cultures should aspire?

This usage is what analysts refer to as "high culture," in that it achieves the highest and best humanity is capable of.

Broadening our scope, one of Webster's definitions for culture is the following: "The customary beliefs, social forms, and material traits of a racial, religious, or social group; also: the characteristic features of everyday existence (as diversions or a way of life) shared by people in a place or time."[1]

In other words, culture operates on both a macro and micro scale, and is all-encompassing.

The Five Ws of Culture

There is always a *who, what, when, where* and *why* involved in any form of cultural expression. Take graffiti, for example. If you are riding a train into New York City, one way to tell you are getting close is by the colorful images and lettering that begin to adorn the barrier walls and industrial buildings on the city outskirts. The bright swirls of color contrast sharply with the drab urban exterior of gray structures and pale sidewalks.

Perhaps you find graffiti repulsive—a scourge, which, like litter, ruins an otherwise impressive cityscape. People consider graffiti to be everything from flagrant vandalism to an accomplished art form. Whatever your reaction, this phenomenon is the product of a specific cultural milieu. Let's take graffiti and consider all five Ws connected to it as a way of understanding the deep origins that a cultural expression has.

What: Graffiti

From the sloppy defacement of a road sign to elaborate twenty-foot-tall paintings, street art is a major feature of urban centers in America and around the world.

Where: City Centers

Although graffiti can occur anywhere, urban graffiti typically decorates the neighborhoods of the individuals who create it. It can be territorial in nature, and may even be tied to gang culture, signifying the importance of status in a place in which the inhabitants often feel there is "no way out."

Who: Anonymous

The anonymity of graffiti is possibly its most intriguing aspect—what lends it its power. After all, if the identities of the artists or perpetrators were discovered, they would likely be arrested. So, the anonymity of the "who" speaks volumes. It speaks of those who are often invisible to mainstream society—those who have no influence—and who therefore create graffiti as a way to assert their presence among us.

Why: Inequity

If someone chooses to draw on public property or others' property, they are presumably making the statement that they have nothing of their own to draw on. No expensive materials, no art lessons, no tools of refinement. In fact, even wealthy, professionally trained artists often turn to street art as a way of saying to the mainstream artistic community that art is not something the establishment should try to control. The "why" of graffiti—the fact that it is on the outside of buildings and not the inside; the fact that it is able to be viewed for free—is a central reason behind its existence.

When: "Now"

Ancient Greek and Roman cultures had graffiti, as did the Mayan and Viking cultures. Its appearance on the contemporary American scene seems to be linked to the cultural unrest of the sixties with the hippie movement and protests against the Vietnam War.

Graffiti can be linked to social unrest, and even to specific political movements. Graffiti is current—a reflection of what is happening now. It is easily painted

> Culture is everywhere, but it comes from somewhere and believes something.

over when a new idea needs to be expressed. Graffiti has an anti-establishment or even anarchist undertone. It exists as a response to a perceived need to tear down prevailing ideologies, such as capitalism.

From this very cursory study of street art, we can see issues of ownership and control motivating the cartoonish characters we so often walk by without even noticing. Culture is everywhere, but it comes from somewhere and believes something.

Nowadays, one hears a lot about "corporate culture," meaning the way a specific organization operates, which differentiates it from the competition. Corporations such as Apple, Facebook and Southwest Airlines have become known for their corporate cultures. They have gained popularity due, in part, to their innovative, relaxed, think-outside-the-box approaches to doing business. Consumers are often attracted to these organizations and their products simply because of how they incorporate their creative or customer service philosophies into what they do.

Are all cultures created equal? And if not, what is the formula to determine which are ideal?

But no one would care how companies went about their business if they did not first feel certain intrinsic needs—reasons why things should be done in a certain way. For instance, Southwest Airlines addresses a need many people feel to be treated as equals; to be treated in a fair way without having to put up with status games and unnecessary red tape surrounding their travel experience.

We are addressing in this book, of course, things of much greater import than the airline someone flies on or the type of laptop someone owns. We are taking a deep, thoughtful gaze into what it means to live in a culture. To return us to our original quest, however, I must steer us back to the question of what a perfect world (or at least an ideal culture) would look like.

Are all cultures created equal? And if not, what is the formula to determine which are ideal?

What Is Normal?

Although we can be sure that Abraham Maslow—an influential professor of developmental psychology working in the mid-twentieth century—did not see the Walgreens commercial about Perfect, U.S.A., I believe he nonetheless asked himself the same question I did: "What would a perfect world be like?" More exactly, "What conditions are necessary for individuals to grow in an ideal way? What does personal life or human society look like when it is allowed to develop to its full potential?"

At the time, many other formative scientists in the field of psychology were focusing their research on just the opposite—studying what a person or group of people look like when something has gone wrong. They studied acute and chronic mental illnesses, as well as societal dysfunction, in an attempt to better understand the human condition.

Maslow, however, suggested that we look at what happens when we thrive—what we can become when we are not battling chemical imbalance, abusive situations or other adverse conditions. Maslow went to the cream of the crop—the best and the brightest—those who contributed in enormous ways to the world around them. He systematically determined what factors were involved in producing such successful, well-adjusted people. His work laid the foundation for what is commonly called the positive psychology movement, which is increasingly popular today. Let's take a brief look at his theory to see what environmental causes produce "ideal" individuals, then we will be able to determine how to achieve a healthy culture comprised of successful, well-adjusted people.

Picture a pyramid divided horizontally into five different sections. Each section represents a category of needs that all people can identify with. The bottom sections are naturally wider and include more basic life needs essential for existence. The higher, narrower sections represent more elusive features. The crux of the theory is that, only when the more foundational needs of people are met can they move up to the next level.

Here is an estimation of Maslow's hierarchy of needs, starting from the bottom of the pyramid and progressing to the top.

1. *Physiological needs:* We first need to have our fundamental, corporeal needs met (such as the need for food and water).
2. *Safety needs:* We feel the need to arrange for our safety both physically and financially. We work to achieve stability in these areas by securing our own well-being.

3. *The need for love and belonging:* We need to be accepted into a social network that satisfies our innate need for intimacy among friends and family.
4. *The need for esteem:* We need to feel a sense of self-esteem and confidence and also recognition that we are making a difference in the world around us.
5. *The need for self-actualization and transcendence:* If we are able to achieve all these needs, we are free to fully flourish and become all we are capable of. At this point, we are also able to eclipse our own egos and become ones who serve others, helping them reach their potential as well.

I am not in any way endorsing Maslow's theory as faultless. It is certainly not. Nor am I agreeing with all of his premises or the conclusions he drew from his research. The reason I present it in our discussion is because I believe this theory provides us with a basic framework for understanding what it means to be human. It gives us a paradigm for understanding common, or "normal," human needs.

What aspirations and desires can be found within us all? Is there a common sense of purpose we are all instinctively working toward? Are there "big questions" in life we are all trying to answer? In other words, if culture is the working out of the inner life of individuals into a corporate milieu, what are the driving needs we individuals seek to satisfy?

The Questions of Culture

- Where do we come from?
- Why am I here?
- Does anyone care about me?
- What should I do with the rest of my life?
- How do I make sense of what I see around me?

If these questions are universal, which they seem to be, it is logical to conclude that cultures either aid or detract us from this pursuit. I firmly believe that the validity of a culture can be determined, in part, by how well it enables individuals within it to meaningfully answer these questions for themselves.

People have basic, intrinsic needs. To fulfill those existential needs, they will look for beliefs—be it belief in the divine or belief in something else. That quest will have a great deal of impact on what becomes of the prevailing "culture" of the town, city or nation. And despite what you may have been taught in American public high school, some cultures are simply better than others.

Ryan Dobson, son of James and Shirley Dobson of Focus on the Family fame, had an interesting title to a book of his. It is humorous, but the point is well taken: *Be Intolerant: Because Some Things Are Just Stupid.*[2]

Funny. A little brash. But a point to consider nonetheless.

When we consider cultures around the world, as we continue to hope and look for a "perfect" or "ideal" culture, let us not fail to state clearly that some cultures are inherently better for people than others. *Better how?* How do we measure good or better or worse when it comes to culture? Are we debating the contributions they have made to the world? Is it simply a matter of who has the best food? Architecture? Sports? Music?

There are certainly many criteria that could be considered in this conversation. I would propose, however, that the most central element of evaluating culture should not merely be judging what it produces, but on how it responds to the basic needs common to humanity. How does a culture or society or belief system view the individual? What rights do they have? Do they have intrinsic worth or are they a commodity? This will determine how individuals are treated.

Returning to our three houses, we can begin to see that each has its own intolerance of the other. How each processes and manifests words, feelings and actions must be understood. Each does have an understanding of its own peculiar right to exist and right to judge others. Each claims to have truth and to be able to think and make decisions objectively. Our mission is to weigh their claims and decide which house is most habitable. Again, they are . . .

• The house of Radical Islam
• The house of Militant Secularism
• The house of the Judeo-Christian worldview

Relatively Speaking

In the first few lines of this book, we considered HSBC's "different values" ad campaign. You remember—three identical images, each with a different word describing the image. I used this real-life example to illustrate how there can be (at least) three very different ways to view the world.

Now, instead of taking the ad campaign at face value, I want to take this illustration one step further. I want to show you how the bank is using the social value of multiculturalism to appeal to a target demographic. You see, upon closer inspection, the bank is exploiting a trendy cultural relativism to score points with potential investors.

The hidden message behind the ad campaign is that everyone's beliefs carry equal weight. HSBC is sending a message that whatever your perspective, whatever your worldview, it is valid (and financeable) simply because you believe it. Someone who possesses a relativistic mind-set might say, "Perspective is everything!" with a shrug of the shoulders. It is precisely this kind of relativism that is decimating our cultural groundwork and values. While it is true that people all over the world embrace a broad spectrum of values, it does not follow that all perspectives are morally sound, critically objective or absolutely true.

Now, do not get confused. I am not saying that others are not entitled to their own opinions. What I am saying is that validating others' opinions, when they are inherently toxic, is a very dangerous thing to do. What about someone who does not believe that jumping off the top of the Empire State Building is a fatal endeavor? Are they correct? Of course not. The laws of physics will prove them wrong.

> Validating others' opinions, when they are inherently toxic, is a very dangerous thing to do.

Exposing the danger of relying on perceptions without giving due weight and proper scrutiny to what shapes those perceptions is one of the objectives of this book. In a world careening from one crisis to the next, it is not difficult to show why we need to more deeply scrutinize the various movements fighting for global ascendancy. They must be analyzed in order to reveal their motivations and, ultimately, the truth behind them. I believe we are being called with greater urgency than ever before to think more critically and search more deeply for the source of the evils that plague our world. Instead of following our perceptions, we need to follow sound wisdom. Wisdom upholds the perspective that holds up under the weight of evidence. It encourages us to base our decisions on that which can stand on its own, without relying on mere opinion.

Culture exists and is measurable. There is a who, what, when, where and why inherent in even the most perfunctory cultural expressions. We can judge the veracity of a culture based on the way in which it treats all manner of individuals that make up its population.

So let us delve next into the most central part of our journey together—an examination of the three dominant cultural kingdoms shaping our world today. As we do this, keep in mind this standard of measure: *Revelation*—not Reason—becomes the ultimate source for knowing absolute truth and making objective decisions. We must free ourselves of a Western mind-set shaped by René Decartes who argued existentially, "*I think, therefore I am.*" He postulated that once the mind was stripped of everything it could doubt, we would arrive at foundational truths that could *not* be doubted. What he used to do the stripping, however, was the fallible tool of human reason, and we find ourselves doing that as well, being products of Western culture.

> We can judge the veracity of a culture based on the way in which it treats all manner of individuals.

Humankind's five basic needs prompt him to search for a house—that is, a mind-set—in which to live. Revealed truth, the foundation for the real world, will provide the light for examining the rooms of each house. Let us begin our search.

4

The Three Houses

n 1996, Samuel P. Huntington of Harvard University released an expansive, seminal work entitled *The Clash of Civilizations and the Remaking of World Order.* In it he set forth a geopolitical view that pointed to civilizations—not nation-states or even world superpowers—as the entities that are contending for supremacy on the world's stage. Huntington cited the influence of cultural differences held by these civilizations as the key to understanding global conflicts and the future of world politics.[1]

The reason this concept is so vitally important is that cultural stances are absolutely pivotal to our understanding both the present-day reality we live in and future global realities. The *cultures* (not the nations) that are at war in the earth today impact and determine the way people will vote, who will go to war with whom, where ethnic groups will immigrate and so forth. If history is any indication, these cultures will continue to shape the course of world events in the days to come, and they will continue to be in conflict.

Culture Clashes

The houses of Radical Islam, Militant Secularism and the Judeo-Christian worldview, though not the only "houses" in existence, are uniquely engaged in a colossal battle—a struggle that ultimately does not allow them to coexist with one another. My hypothesis is that these three prevailing worldviews are all, in different yet equally serious ways, seeking the hearts, souls, minds and bodies of mankind. The end game is to emerge as the dominant player, allowing them to influence and even redefine the future of human existence.

By no means do all who find themselves within one of these houses subscribe to all (or even most) of the tenets that the overall worldview sets forth. In the house of Islam, for instance, there is much variation in the particulars of Islamic beliefs and in the level of fervency with which those beliefs are espoused. For this reason, it is common to refer to certain circles as moderate, or to talk about Shia Islam v. Sunni Islam, or to highlight the cultural differences from one nation to another. The same is true of Secularism, which encompasses an extremely diverse and often contradictory set of beliefs. The Judeo-Christian world also has been far from unified for much of its history. As in any society, there is an architecture that determines each house's structure, and these three world powers are no exception. Our job is to discover what are the prevailing thoughts, attitudes, individuals and movements that guide the architects of each house. As we do so, it will become clear that the dominant system within each of these houses puts it in direct conflict with the others.

In contrast with the ancient world, in which ethnic and religious clashes had more to do with competing people groups vying for resources such as land, the twentieth century saw a new type of conflict emerge: ideological warfare. A war of ideas. As global systems became more advanced, and the basic needs of humanity became better accommodated on the whole, people were free to delve deeper into their belief systems as well as attempt to impose them on others.

While it is not inherently problematic to share personal convictions with someone else, and even win them over, the problem comes when the system at hand is a brutal regime intent on subjugating everything and everyone under its repressive philosophy.

The twentieth century saw a new type of conflict emerge: ideological warfare.

Two of the most prominent paradigms to have vied for the hearts of humanity within the last century are European Fascism and Soviet Communism. These cultural forces required, respectively, a gory world war and an extended cold war to die out. As these two former superpowers proved, ideological warfare can have dire physical consequences. Because of the power-hungry nature of supremacist despots, they stop at nothing in pursuit of their goals. They know that the more power they gain, the less they will have to answer to any objective standards upholding intrinsic human worth. Anything is justifiable. In Hitler's words, "The tears of war will produce the daily bread for the generations to come."[2]

There is, however, another much more primal level of confrontation on which ideological warfare operates—the battlefield of the mind. The apostle Paul was familiar with the first-century clash of cultures, understanding clearly the streams of rabbinical Jewish thought, Greek and Roman philosophy and political reasoning, as well as the dynamics of revelatory truth. He wrote this to the believers at Corinth:

> For the weapons of our warfare are not carnal but mighty in God for pulling down strongholds, casting down arguments

and every high thing that exalts itself against the knowledge of God, bringing every thought into captivity to the obedience of Christ, and being ready to punish all disobedience when your obedience is fulfilled.

2 Corinthians 10:4–6

The Greek concept of stronghold (Greek: *ochuroomatos*) is a military derivative referring to a castle, fortress or anything upon which one relies for protection and defense. In modern thought, we might think of a stronghold as the ego's defense mechanism to protect one's inner self from any outside attack that would threaten one's core beliefs, spiritual or ethical values, worldview or mind-set. Anything in a worldview that opposes God's absolute truth will create in the mind a stronghold that resists change, transformation or obedience to Christ. A spiritual battlefield is created in the mind. Today, this battlefield becomes the arena in which armies of ideas from the opposing houses war against the Judeo-Christian worldview.

As we have covered, the day in which we live truly marks "the end of the world as we know it." Not only is the world a vastly different place from what it was even for our grandparents, many feel that the degree of unrest in virtually every corner of the planet will cause its ultimate demise—that is, its metamorphosis into something radically different from what we know as the world today. We stand at present in the unfolding of a whole new era in world history, one in which "business as usual" is far from a guaranteed reality.

In 1999, I wrote a book called *Prepare the Way*, which dealt with the changing landscape of evangelical Christianity at the brink of the new millennium. Even in the short time since the writing of that book, an untold number of geopolitical and societal changes have taken place, confirming that the rapid change around us will only accelerate in years ahead. If we are to be effective in this world as Christians, Jews or people of any faith who genuinely believe in basic, individual freedoms and in goodwill toward others, we must recognize the current state of affairs for what it is. We must see how it both drastically differs from and simultaneously resembles the centuries preceding us. We must be both students of history and makers of history.

Jesus: Then and Now

Two millennia ago, a man named Jesus was born in a small Middle Eastern town in a land promised by God to His forebears, the Jewish nation. Called an influential philosopher by some, a rebel by others and a Savior by still more, this Jesus was born into a world dominated by a formidable empire, which came on the heels of Greek and Hellenistic rulership. Some called Jesus' teachings new; others recognized the Jewish roots from which they were drawn. The people of Israel had suffered greatly at the hands of their oppressors, and much of the population looked to Jesus as a rabbi from their own Jewish community, who read their Torah Scriptures and walked their streets, and who could deliver them from subjugation to the Romans. What-

> **We must be both students of history and makers of history.**

ever people thought of Him then, the way of life Jesus offered has made a profound impact on virtually every human society since.

Man's struggle for global domination, which the Romans had won for the moment, would soon be up for grabs once again. Roman emperors like Augustus and Nero and Marcus Aurelius could not have known how much a simple Jewish carpenter's influence would endure, long after Rome and its own vast domains fell in the fifth century. Ironically, this humble Rabbi's teachings spread from His followers to become the majorly influential world power known as Christendom.

Christianity, which has existed as a matter of personal conviction and a means of altruistic societal betterment, as well as a political force wielded to exert control, hails from God's dealings with an ancient tribe of desert nomads known as the Hebrews and their Mosaic Law, the Ten Commandments.

In the days of the superpower Roman Empire, which at its height spanned from present-day England to Iraq,[3] both traditional Judaism and the rapidly multiplying followers of Christ were brutally persecuted. This resulted in the Jewish *Diaspora* (dispersion) and also the eventual spread of Christianity throughout the known world. In the early fourth century, the emperor Constantine, to suit his own religious and political ends, sought to drive a wedge between the two expressions of faith in favor of his own adaptation of Christianity.

Ironically, while the split between the two sister faiths of Judaism and Christianity widened into a deep and painful rift, Constantine's actions played a significant role in causing the Judeo-Christian worldview as a whole to supersede his own empire, under the powerful kingpin of Christendom. Jews and Christians were acutely divided to the point of extreme, sustained persecution of Jews by Christians. Nevertheless, they were not to be separated forever, as more recent history has proved. Even when apart, both faith communities continued to hold fast to a worldview that deeply honored the Scriptures.

That trust in the veracity of the Scriptures has resulted today in a reconciled Jewish-Christian relationship that has emerged stronger than ever. The unprecedented birth of evangelical Christian groups such as the International Christian Embassy Jerusalem, Bridges for Peace, Christians United for Israel and many others has served to unite millions of Christians around the world with their Jewish brothers and sisters. This embrace of Israel has also been a strong emphasis in the Roman Catholic Church, particularly since Pope Paul VI and the *Nostra Aetate* ("In Our Time") declaration of Vatican II in 1965, which was an act of repentance on behalf of the Catholic faith for accusations it had harbored against the Jewish people.[4]

Because of Jews' and Christians' spiritual foundation and faith heritage in the God of the Bible, the living expression of this house has always emphasized blessing for the entire sum of humanity, as was foretold in the days of the Hebrew Old Testament prophets ("I will make you as a light for the nations," Isaiah 49:6, ESV). The Judeo-Christian house has also always faced persecution throughout its history. What is even more surprising is that a large portion of this persecution has come at the hand of Islam, which traces its roots back to the same father that Jews and Christians do: the patriarch Abraham.

> The Judeo-Christian house has also always faced persecution throughout its history.

Muhammad: Then and Now

Less than one hundred years after the fall of the last emperor of the Western Roman Empire (A.D. 476), Muhammad ibn 'Abdullāh was born in the Arabian Peninsula. Like Jesus, he too was a teacher whose philosophies were perceived as both new and old. And though his early years of leadership were fraught with much opposition, he eventually gained a following, largely through violence, and became a major player in the global arena.

The rise of Islam from the seventh century on yielded a formidable obstacle to the spread of the Judeo-Christian worldview. The radical Islamic ideology, as we will explore in a later chapter, leaves no room for those who oppose it. And Islam, within a few centuries of its inception, set its sights on Christians and Jews with a fierceness that was as pronounced as it was swift. Throughout the Middle Ages, militant Muslim conquests and the defensive response of the Crusades of Christendom spread across Europe, Africa and the Middle East, violently spilling much blood over the lands they ravaged. Among the ferocious battles that took place was the attack on the Byzantine city of Constantinople in 1453 (in Asia Minor, which is modern-day Turkey). Muslims captured and then renamed the city Istanbul. Turkey has remained a key Islamic post even after the fall of the Ottoman Empire and in its current relationship with the present-day European Union.

This is a brief glance at the foundation of what has come to be known as Radical Islam. A myriad of prevailing voices since—including Daniel Pipes, Bat Ye'or, Brigitte Gabriel, Mosab Hassan Yousef, Walid Shoebat, Nonie Darwish and Joel Rosenberg, to name a few—have pointed to radical Islamic civilization as a powerful, polarizing influence in the 21st century. Gifted thinkers have made this argument from both a scholastic and an experiential standpoint. The phenomenon of Radical Islam has been agreed upon by moderate Muslims, like M. Zuhdi Jasser of the American Islamic Forum for Democracy, as well as those outside the Muslim faith. The radical Islamists themselves, who have in practice clearly chosen to set themselves against the idea of peacefully living alongside those of non-Muslim beliefs, have, sadly, proven the vicious and volatile nature of this house.

One of the rising groups among Muslim Palestinians has been Hamas (or the Islamic Resistance Movement), internationally known as a terrorist organization, originating from the Muslim Brotherhood movement in Egypt, and waging an intensifying warfare against Israel. Since their 2006 election victory in the Palestinian territories (including Gaza), Hamas has married political activity to its avowed methods of violence. The charter of Hamas explicitly shows the violent intent that characterizes this radical Muslim ideology:

> The Islamic Resistance Movement erupted in order to play its role in the path of its Lord. In so doing, it joined its hands with those of all Jihad fighters for the purpose of liberating Palestine. . . . It will need all the loyal efforts we can wield, to be followed by further steps and reinforced by successive battalions from

the multifarious Arab and Islamic world, until the enemies are defeated and Allah's victory prevails.[5]

From a demographic standpoint, the growth of both Christianity and Islam has tremendously accelerated since their beginnings, intensifying the ideological clash that is currently taking place between them. The far reaches of these systems of thought cannot be adequately measured; they have taken hold in every continent. Of the major world religions today, Christianity (including all denominations and sects) ranked first with 33 percent of the world's population (approximately 2.1 billion), and Islam ranked second with 21 percent (approximately 1.5 billion).[6] While Christianity still has an edge over Islam in numbers of adherents, Islam's growth rate has been rising astronomically due to high birthrates. Statistics reveal that Islam will match, if not overtake, Christianity in the next several decades if current trends continue.[7]

Political scientist Samuel Huntington highlighted the importance of this battle in *The Clash of Civilizations,* pointing out that for present-day competing cultures, it is not principally the individual borders and territories of nations that are at stake. Rather, it is the future of the international social climate and global political supremacy that hang in the balance. His description of Islamic civilization is that "throughout Islam the small group and the great faith, the tribe and the *ummah* [worldwide Muslim community], have been the principal foci of loyalty and commitment, and the nation state has been less significant."[8] Because of this reality, in Huntington's pre-9/11 work, he was already questioning the invincibility of the West by citing that Islam is not enamored with the secular approach to commercial influence that has captured the hearts of America and Europe. Islam has a different battle plan coming from a different school of thought—one rooted in tribal customs and a staunchly Muslim identity—and it is actively at war with the West.

The Kingdom of Us

Not to be discounted, however, is the influence seen from global-ization: secular humanism's kingdom. Perhaps the least obvious of the three houses at first glance, Militant Secularism is nevertheless one of the most influential forces you will ever encounter in your life. With its irreligious, amoral veneer, militant secular humanism may have won the most "converts" of all; and there appears to be no end in sight. In terms of numbers, secularists, non-religious people and atheists come in third place, just behind Christianity and Islam, accounting for 16 percent of the world's population (approximately 1.1 billion).[9]

> Islam is not enamored with the secular approach to commercial influence that has captured the hearts of America and Europe.

From the days of the Greek philosophers and even before, secular humanism—the declaration of materialism over spiritu-ality and humankind's infinite ability to master his own fate—has had a prevalent role in pre-Western and current Western culture. The original idea of democracy comes from the Greek societal concept of a *polis* ("city" or "city-state"), which was developed under the assumption that humankind could rule itself autonomously. Even the sculptures of the ancient Greeks evidenced this humanism, glorifying the human body by em-phasizing perfect proportional form. While Judeo-Christian thought values the worth of the individual and sees each person as uniquely formed in the image of God, it does not glorify the creature; rather, the Creator is glorified.

In the wake of the Crusades, Europe turned a new page through the work of religious reformations, technological innovations and the Age of Exploration. This new wave of creativity spread farther west to parts of the globe previously unknown to majority popu-lations. This chapter of mankind's story marked monumental (though not always admirable) advances in human civilization. In the period of time known as the Enlightenment (in full swing by the eighteenth century), the idea of self-realization apart from God—inspired by the Greeks—reached a new level. The leading thinkers of the day scoffed at the idea of faith, and man's reason developed a logical argument against God. If God existed at all, He was more of a distant, unknowable Being—possibly the world's Creator, but for all intents and purposes, irrelevant.

When the age of information, innovation, humanities and technology dawned from the Renaissance period onward, secularism led the charge by capitalizing on man's inner need to discover and invent solutions through creative thinking. Free market capitalism added fuel to the fire of man's search for individual significance, and a proliferation of this worldview went global at a truly astonishing pace. Pride in our tremendous abilities had become a contender for the souls of men on the world's stage through a Darwinian-based ideology of its own.

Initially this house of thought only traveled with those who walked, rode horses or sailed the high seas. But in recent decades, secularism has been transmitted not only with the help of airplanes but also cell phones, websites, chat rooms, webinars, blogs, tweets, Facebook posts, DVDs, MP3s and every type of electronic media people have been able to dream up. Although each house and arguably the majority of the people on the planet use these media, the secular kingdom "owns" them, in that it thrives on turning us into consumers who must depend upon the newest, fastest, smartest gadgets to keep up with the rest of the world.

> Pride in our tremendous abilities had become a contender for the souls of men.

The rampant, global nature of secularism is causing Western religious groups to divorce themselves from their roots to be more socially acceptable in the connected world. Just recently, the Young

Women's Christian Association (YWCA) in England announced that it was removing the word "Christian" from its name, opting to identify the charity now as "Platform 51," after the 51 percent of the global population that is female. Their stated goal is a universal appeal to help make the voice of all women heard.[10] Apparently, in the present day of globalization, even established names are on the chopping block in the midst of the battle.

Let's recap. What I am proposing is that from the stage of world history have arisen three primary *houses of thought,* three perspectives of the world, three cultural kingdoms that are currently contending for global ascendancy: Radical Islam, Militant Secularism and the Judeo-Christian worldview. They are not the *only* three houses in existence today, but as we survey the landscape of global affairs, we see that their pervasiveness is uncontestable, and their shaping influence beyond doubt. As "houses" they are the ideological structures in which thoughts of a certain kind grow to maturity. They are also the foundational residences from which those who call them their home subsequently act upon those systems of thought.

Absolute Opposition

There is one more ray of light I would like to shed on our topic before we move on to our discussion of the three houses. Like the historical context we just discussed, this knowledge is essential to our understanding of how the residents of these houses will continue to interact. This conversation is one of absolutes.

As we talked about in the last chapter, humanity is hardwired with certain core needs and objectives. There are certain questions we grapple with in every culture, every geography, every generation. *How did we get here? Were we created? Why are we here? Are there eternal consequences for my actions? Is there a divine architect watching over all that is happening? What happens when we die?*

Religious systems offer a code of moral absolutes that provide answers to such questions. God's Word will tell you how to ensure your eternal salvation through faith in Jesus Christ; Allah offers a free pass to anyone willing to kill themselves and take others with them in the process. Even Hinduism will let you know what you have coming to you in your next life based on how you have behaved in this one. These belief systems encompass the idea that there is a fixed reality from which is derived a system of moral law. Furthermore, this morality has consequences for everyone—whether or not any given person chooses to acknowledge and live by it. In other words, these systems believe themselves to be like a train leaving the station at six o'clock sharp. If you are on it, great; if not, you are stuck, because there is not another one coming.

> In absolutist systems, there is a fixed conception of right and wrong by which individuals will be judged.

We like to believe and hope for transcendent values shared by all religions—attributes like love, forgiveness, care for the poor and respect for elders. While there may (or may not) be shared values in different religious systems, there are unquestionably great differences in the moral codes of various faiths. The thing common to them all, however, is a sense of moral imperative—a moral "ought." In absolutist systems, there is a fixed conception of right and wrong by which individuals will be judged. Whether that judgment comes from Allah or Christ or Jehovah or karma, there is a place of absolute right and wrong and an accounting for one's deeds, either in this life or the next.

Atheists, agnostics and the like would look at the contradictions between these and other religious beliefs and argue that this proves there could be no absolute principles governing our lives; no definitive answers. This line of reasoning postulates that, since absolute consequences cannot be measured or easily proven, it is better to do away with them altogether and accept that "right" and "wrong" are merely social constructs defined only on a case-by-case basis by those who arbitrate them.

In contrast with Islam and the Judeo-Christian ethic, humanism (the house of Militant Secularism) represents a non-absolutist worldview. It offers no system of moral absolutes. It is a relativistic paradigm that attempts to develop morality from the situation at hand, relative to the needs and wants of the individual perspectives involved. When survival of the fittest is one's central value, Christian concepts such as "denying yourself" (see Matthew 16:24) or "laying down your life for your friends" (see John 15:13) sound absurd—even mad!

So too, militant secularists misinterpret the absolutist ultimatums of Islam. To those who do not believe in good and evil, the actions of suicide bombers and Holocaust-deniers do not register for what they are. The problem intensifies when these moral relativists attempt to interpret such actions and movements through their own, non-absolutist lens. They naively reason there must be valid social factors motivating this behavior. Poverty is the most common explanation this rationale has to offer. When everything is relative to circumstance, there is always a way of justifying any action, however heinous.

So, how does the fact that there are both absolutist and non-absolutist systems of thought influencing mankind affect our study of the three houses? In many ways. We will return to this question after we have taken an in-depth look at these worldviews. But for now, I want to make one final point.

It seems obvious to me that world populations will become increasingly polarized as the staggering number of catastrophic events we are bombarded with continue to unfold upon our planet. Wars that show no sign of stopping, natural disasters that strike with mounting force, human malevolence and irresponsibility that sabotage economies—the world is not a friendly place to live. As things continue to go from bad to worse, the clashes we hear about on the nightly news will only continue to worsen as everyone reevaluates what he or she believes and determines to hold to it more rigorously in the face of unrelenting challenges. Whatever people choose to believe, they are going to believe it with more fervor than ever. Naturally, the composition of the world will become more and more polarized to the point of utter incompatibility.

> Whatever people choose to believe, they are going to believe it with more fervor than ever.

Of course I am not the only person noticing this. The polarization debate has been going on for a while now. Those who would attempt to deny the effects of polarization are hard-pressed to find evidence. Really, their disagreement about polarization is more a criticism of it than a convincing dispute over its existence. They ridicule or dismiss as extremist any who refuse to throw in the towel on absolutes and join them in their relativistic, "anything goes" malaise. They insist that people are not, in actuality, drifting toward polar extremes. Are they correct, or is their argument really just a way for them to gain leverage? The question becomes, Will the magnetic pull of either of the two opposing absolutist houses (Radical Islam and Judeo-Christianity) be strong enough to draw people out from the cavernous abyss of moral equivocation in between? Or, alternatively, will the house of Militant Secularism absorb the searching multitudes into its black hole of relativism?

Three Houses under One Roof

We are about to continue on in our journey by examining how impossible it is for these opposing worldviews to exist harmoniously. As we do, I want you to have a clear image of the three houses emblazoned in your memory, so I am going to leave you with a story that will do just that.

Just recently, I was involved with commissioning a team of exceptional young people to embark on a special assignment to York University in Toronto, Canada, a few short hours from my ministry base in New York State. The trip was prompted by the anti-Israel bias and protests taking place on campus during "Israel Apartheid Week," which is an assault on the Jewish people based on counter-factual information equating Israeli policies to that of Apartheid South Africa.

In keeping with the Judeo-Christian worldview, this small group of college-aged believers (in their twenties) went to this campus (which is the size of a small city) with the goal of lifting up the name of Jesus and declaring their support of Israel. The young people undertaking this assignment knew it would not be easy, but the clash of contending cultures was enough to make them, who regularly work with undergraduates and who are already well aware of these issues, balk in disbelief. As the team prepared for a time of worship and prayer, which a student had invited them to lead inside the university's new religious center, they experienced a face-to-face encounter with the houses of Radical Islam and secular humanism.

Just beyond the thin walls and set of doors, our humble song and prayer service was literally surrounded by a circle of young Muslim men bowing on prayer rugs toward Mecca. Young women in full burkas were using special Muslim-only bathrooms to do their ceremonial washings before prayers—a reminder of how far this ideology has encroached upon Western civilization.

As all this was going on, one of our team members noticed a provocative poster above a hallway water fountain advertising emergency contraception (the "morning-after pill"). The poster showed a microscopic image of sperm cells heading toward a female ovum with a one-word question appearing above it: "Screwed?" So, in the midst of this charged atmosphere of potent spiritual contention, the house of Militant Secularism was also present, with its message of self-centered gratification vying for young, impressionable souls.

Although this interaction may evidence a cataclysmic struggle at work in the earth, we would do well to remind ourselves that it is also typical, continuous and, for lack of a better word, *normal*. The setting in which this story took place is an everyday experience for most high school or college students today.

Is Harmony Possible?

In a democratic culture, the ideal would be for peaceful harmony and tolerance to prevail. The very nature of a democracy, however, functions under the principle of *majority rules*. Knowing this, the house of Radical Islam seeks to so populate the culture through immigration and birthrate that a majority is created and eventually Sharia law governs the culture. The house of Militant Secularism uses the educational systems and media to influence the thinking of the upcoming generation so that it becomes the majority and thereby controls the mind-sets of the legislators. What are those in the house of the Judeo-Christian worldview to do?

Christians must use the democratic platform for freedom of expression to speak the truth in love—at every opportunity living out their faith, being salt and light in the culture and manifesting godly character in government, media, the arts, religious settings, education, business and finance. Jesus admonished His followers to be a light on a hill and not to hide or retreat (see Matthew 5). America was founded by Christian believers to be that "city on a hill."

Yes, such activity will be attacked and ridiculed by the other two houses. The battle for the minds and souls of citizens will be unremitting, requiring tremendous sacrifices of time, resources and energy. In the end, we have the sure hope that truth will eventually prevail. Truth is what can set us free from tyranny and fanaticism, just as John Hus, George Washington, Samuel Adams, Abraham Lincoln and countless others—including Jesus—proclaimed.

Now we must turn our attention to how a myth of harmony and coexistence among these houses should be addressed and demythologized.

5

The Myth of Coexistence

am about to tell you something that you've heard a thousand times before . . . first, in a Sunday morning preschool class; more recently on T-shirts or proclaimed from street corner preachers handing out tracts. The catchphrase I'm referring to is *God is love*.

I believe with all my heart that the Creator of the universe is a God of infinite, extraordinary, compassionate, everlasting, unfathomable, indescribable love. It is always there, always available, always close—not just for a few lucky ones, but for whoever is willing to give it a try.

God loves. That's it! Period. He *loves*. That is what He does. All day. Every day. Forever. It is His breath. His nature. His essence.

Whom does He love? Everyone. Absolutely everyone. No holds barred. No fine print.

Christians, Jews, Muslims, Hindus, Buddhists, Baptists, atheists, botanists. Democrats, Communists, Canadians, secretaries. Lindsay Lohan, Pat Robertson, the guy from the Verizon Wireless commercials. The life-all-together types and the life-all-messed-up types. Me. You. Her. Him. Us. Them. Everyone. From Mother Teresa to Moammar Gadhafi, God loves us all.

This is at the core of my belief system, and I attempt to live it every day. It grieves me that so many today see those of us with a firm belief in the God of the Bible as angry, small-minded, nasty people. Many think Christians view God primarily as angry, vengeful and eager to punish. This is not the case, and I'm sure God would be as perplexed at this description of Himself as He must be at being blamed for every natural disaster that comes along.

> **From Mother Teresa to Moammar Gadhafi, God loves us all.**

God made us all (and in His own image, at that!). How could He *not* love His creation? Because of this I endeavor, as we all should, to treat everyone—even those with whom we adamantly disagree—with the utmost dignity and respect.

Because we hear so much of this *God is love* message, it's easy to write it off as a nice sentiment, but one that couldn't possibly mean anything practical for our lives. Even if we accept it as true, do we really understand its implications? What does the fact that God is love—that He loves us—mean?

Tough Love

I have met a lot of people, as I am sure you have, who relegate Jesus to the status of a moral philosopher, a well-meaning truth-seeker, a peacenik pushover. While it is true that Jesus did not come to condemn the world, but to save it (see John 3:17), Jesus' arrival onto the scene was an act of war. It was God declaring to Satan and his evil, defective minions the beginning of His intervention that will result in the eventual overthrow of Satan's counterfeit authority.

The act of Jesus giving His life on the cross is representative of the price required to redeem humanity. And the moment He rose from the grave, it was all over. Satan lost the power he seized when he deceived mankind so long ago. Jesus came to set up the eternal Kingdom of the one, true God on earth. He began His ministry by saying, "The time is fulfilled, and the kingdom of God is at hand. Repent, and believe in the gospel" (Mark 1:15). Sure, He did a lot of good deeds, fed and taught a lot of people, and even performed many miracles as an outpouring of the love of God He brought to His people. But the good news He preached was as much a warning to those who would not listen as it was a blessing to those who did.

Because God's love is real, it desires what is really best for us, which is perhaps what distinguishes it from the most well-intentioned human affection:

> Man's love is a love that excuses.
> God's love is a love that redeems.

The Jesus who said "Let the little children come to Me" (Matthew 19:14), the Jesus who embraced the outcasts and spoke kindly to desperate sinners, is the same Jesus who overturned the tables of the corrupt merchants who were fleecing those less fortunate than they. This same Jesus called out the pompous religious hypocrites of His day for what they were.

Jesus clarifies His intent:

> "Do not think that I came to bring peace on earth. I did not come to bring peace but a sword. For I have come to *'set a man against his father, a daughter against her mother, and a daughter-in-law against her mother-in-law'; and 'a man's enemies will be those of his own household.'"*
>
> Matthew 10:34–36 (emphasis added)

The message that brought hope and comfort to those who would receive it also brought formidable results for those who refused.

God is ultimately concerned about the division that sin (separation) causes between humanity and Himself. He wants us to renounce all that is unholy and untrue—all that is not of Him. This severance actually brings a true and lasting unity between us and Him, and among all who believe. This is what the Church was always meant to be—not a cultural club, but a countercultural Kingdom encompassing and unifying all the colors and kinds of God's creation. This is what it will one day be. Until then, we must continue Jesus' ministry of reconciliation until the separation sin causes between us and our Creator is conquered by the redeeming work of Christ.

We should each live in such a way that could be described as loving. But sending someone smiles, cheers and positive reinforcement while what he is doing is about to take him over the edge of a cliff is not the most loving action I can think of. It is in this spirit that I offer to you the reasons I do not buy in to the myth of coexistence.

Intolerant Tolerance

So, here we are, continuing to swim upstream against the widely accepted norms of our day. At the top of this list of societal tripe sits the often well-intentioned notion that we can all "just get along."

This is, of course, exactly the message we are being bombarded with on a constant basis from the other two houses. The militant secularists tell us that the diversity of our ideas is our strength because they really believe that to be so. The radical Islamists infiltrating the Judeo-Christian institutions of Western civilization are telling us the same thing—not because they truly believe it, but because they know it is what we want to hear. (More on this later.) The irony is that the traditional values under assault in this nation are derived from the one genuinely tolerant worldview there is.

Dr. Daniel Juster has done a compelling study on the modern origin of religious liberty, citing it as "one of the most remarkable legacies of the United States."[1] Beginning in the ancient world, Juster shows how religious and governmental order were inseparable. He points out that it was first-century followers of Christ who asserted the idea that Caesar was not Lord, and that their persecution for not sacrificing to temple gods was unfounded.

After the unforeseen anomaly of Christianity becoming a state religion under Constantine, it was not until the seventeenth century, eventually culminating in the writing of the U.S. Constitution, that the revolutionary concept of religious persuasion as a matter of personal choice was secured. To these innovative thinkers, "conscience must not be constrained, because true religion requires freedom of conscience, including the right to seek to persuade others of one's beliefs or lack thereof."[2] Juster goes on to explain that "the founding fathers . . . did not interpret this separation to mean that the state would not acknowledge God's basic law and their accountability to God. It was an institutional separation. It was assumed that a Judeo-Christian framework would be foundational for the state."[3]

In the past few decades, *tolerance* has become the buzzword to end all buzzwords. Political pundits love throwing it around. It is exalted as the key virtue of our day. And really, in many circles, it is the *only* virtue of our day. But the way this word is now used is far from its original intent, and ironically, contradicts it entirely.

A primary meaning for the word *tolerance* (from 1868) describes it as an "allowable amount of variation."[4] This makes sense, considering the root word *tolerate,* which implies there is some measure of disagreement or unpleasantness involved in the matter at hand. One *tolerates* something he or she dislikes or finds offensive. Some examples of this age-old definition:

The medicine disagrees with his system, but he is able to tolerate it in small doses.

She tolerates his actions, but does not approve of them.

So, the essence of tolerance is acknowledging differences or dislikes between two parties, but not denying the right of the other party to operate within bounds. By this definition, it is clear that there are, conversely, some things that should *not* be tolerated. (For instance, tolerating a mass murderer by inviting him to be a guest in your home would be unwise.) To sum up, the actual expression of tolerance would say, "I disagree with you, but will tolerate your opinion nevertheless."

Absurdly, the buzzword definition of tolerance has taken on a completely contradictory meaning to the true definition of tolerance. The self-appointed "tolerance police" are, ironically, doing the opposite of tolerating when they shut those of differing positions out of the conversation. Their stance is that if someone disagrees with them, then that person is intolerant. Thus, they have changed the definition of tolerance from *agreeing to disagree* to meaning that *no one is allowed to disagree* with them.

> They have changed the definition of tolerance from *agreeing to disagree* to meaning that *no one is allowed to disagree* with them.

I'm sure you are familiar with this type of censure in the name of "tolerance." Have you heard of the recent incident involving the Reverend Franklin Graham? The son of renowned evangelist Billy Graham, Franklin was *dis*invited from a service being held at the Pentagon on the National Day of Prayer because of comments he had made about Islam, asserting that, "Muslims are 'enslaved' by their religion."[5] For their part, CAIR (the Council on American Islamic Relations), often accused of back-door

84

agreements with terrorists, chalked this up as another victory in light of the active role they played in petitioning the Pentagon to cancel Reverend Graham.[6]

This brand of tolerance denies anyone the right to say that someone else's opinion, choices or lifestyle is wrong. It goes so far as to censure one for merely having the thought; so it is, by the authentic definition of the word, *in*tolerant.

A similar phenomenon has taken place in recent years surrounding the redefinition and misuse of the term *multiculturalism*. Instead of simply referring to many distinct cultures being equally protected so that they may exist side by side, it has morphed into a political tool, used by those who would seek to gain the upper hand by silencing the voice of traditional morality, which gave multiculturalism its validity in the first place.

Faulty Multiculturalism

When you hear the word *multiculturalism*, do you think of a food court? I bet a lot of people do. Many believe the tantalizing array of delicious foreign cuisine available to us is the best thing about this nation. And it is pretty wonderful. I love the fact that in virtually any city in the United States one can get an excellent Indian meal or tasty Thai all on the same street. The melting pot at its best, right? What could be more American than multiculturalism?

What could be more American than multiculturalism?

The problem is that some who come to these shores do not want to assimilate into a distinctly American standard of conduct, adopting our core values and abiding by the rule of law. The food might be great, but what about the idols, customs and antidemocratic mind-sets that seek to impose their values and beliefs on others? Unfortunately, moral relativists have taken

85

multiculturalism (or diversity) by the hand, and they are using it as a platform to push their own political agendas. Their aim is to erode the Christian foundation that gives stability and viability to our shared life.

This agenda is carried out through groups such as the American Civil Liberties Union (ACLU), which I believe is much less concerned about our civil liberties than it is with advancing a society in which religion is cast out as irrelevant, dangerous and backward. Their religion of non-religion seems more dogmatic and intolerant than much of what I find in enlightened, caring churches across America today. There are so many outrageous examples of this, but here are just a few to give you an idea:

In 2010, the ACLU, along with one other agency, sued a school district in Connecticut for planning to hold high school commencement proceedings in a Baptist church. Two students, claiming that they did not feel comfortable graduating in a church, elected to proceed with the lawsuit even though the school board demonstrated a willingness to cover up religious symbols in the church.[7]

In another ACLU-represented case that gained much national attention, a 29-foot cross displayed in a San Diego park to honor Korean War veterans was ruled unconstitutional in 2011 after 55 years of being on display. This shocking case and others like it aptly demonstrate the present-day assault against any religious affiliation in community life.[8]

If that weren't bad enough, the movement of relativism has moved beyond the realm of religion to also attack established national symbols. It has now become commonplace to order the American flag be removed from personal property if it is "offensive" to neighbors. In separate incidents, a boy in California had to remove the flag from his bicycle,[9] an *army veteran* in Wisconsin had to remove the flag from his apartment window[10] and a woman in Texas had to remove a flag from her office *while commemorating Memorial Day!*[11] This is all happening in *America,* mind you.

In a futile attempt to coexist with those who are avowedly hostile to our values, we have compromised the biblical, Judeo-Christian foundations upon which our nation was built. We need to reclaim the American virtues of tolerance and multiculturalism for what they are and appropriate them in such a way that does not alter the fabric of our society into something unrecognizable, and ultimately lethal.

Some aspects of this new brand of politically correct multiculturalism include:

- Minimizing the concept of there being such a thing as right and wrong. It would have us believe that all expressions of faith and culture are equally true.
- Nullifying the central faith of this nation by keeping it out of the public sphere. (Removing the Ten Commandments from courthouses, educating public school students about minority cultures while forbidding traditional standards to even be expressed.)
- Over-accommodating minority cultures by giving them as much sway as the majority waters down the guiding principles this nation was founded on.

Bumper Sticker Theology

Have you seen the bumper sticker? The word is *coexist*. But rather than being spelled out in normal type, it uses the symbols of various religious or social persuasions to form the letters. The Muslim crescent is the *C*, the Jewish star is the *X*, the Christian cross the *T*, etc. The theme seems nice—a peaceable sentiment. All religions are just one letter in a long chain, which, if linked together, can form meaning and cohesion for society.

It's a nice thought—but is it true? Is it plausible? Let me assure you that if it were, I would be the first one to give a standing ovation. I would be thrilled at the prospect of living in harmony and retiring in my later years without a care in the world. There is, however, a catch to this popular theory—a fatal design flaw. There are several significant reasons why coexistence is not possible among the three contending houses described in this book. We will spend the remainder of our time together discovering why that is, but for now, I would like to outline a few reasons to frame that conversation.

Why Coexistence Is a Myth

1. Coexistence does not allow for a dominant culture.

Superficial coexistence is not attainable because it does not allow for a dominant culture. Without one, true, agreed-upon standard for judging cultural expressions, we find multiculturalism to be a distorted reality that cannot ultimately survive. By default, there must be a dominant culture or house of thought governing any given society, or else nothing will hold it together and it will crumble from lack of cohesion. Not every perspective within that culture must embrace the full extent of the principles by which it is governed; on the contrary, a minority group may even benefit from those governing principles without adopting the full cultural paradigm of the majority. But as long as a benevolent culture is allowed to prevail, its uplifting benefits will guide and protect the everyday life of all its adherents.

> There must be a dominant culture or house of thought governing any given society.

What the dominant culture adopts as its position regarding the existence of God will, for better or worse, set the tone for a whole society. As we will later see, the way some societies view God as violent invariably leads them to promote and commit acts of violence against those of a different mind-set. By contrast, others, like the majority of those in the Judeo-Christian house, understand God to be a God of love, who values the dignity and worth of human beings. Still others spend their lives doing their utmost to eradicate the mention and influence of God in every societal arena.

America, at its core, has been founded and developed within a Judeo-Christian ethos, or worldview. I am not going to debate whether Thomas Jefferson was a Christian (doubtful) or a Deist (probable), but the fact of the matter is there is a plethora of evidence that proves, beyond the shadow of any doubt, that this nation's framework has been based on the moral code of the Judeo-Christian Scriptures. This biblical worldview has framed what we know today as Western civilization—from America to Argentina to Britain to Italy to Australia. And, Israel. But all that is changing.

The triumph of rationalism in France through the Renaissance, French Revolution, economic socialism and existential education has birthed a Militant Secularism that pervades both public and private sectors. Jessica Reed depicts a common mindset in France among the emerging generation: "I am part of the first generation of my French family not to get baptized or be sent to Sunday school and I remain an atheist. I was brought up without religion. . . . By choosing to bring me up this way [my mother] broke new ground. . . . My family seems to have gradually lost faith, or at least lost any sustained interest in it, during the past 25 years."[12]

Polls in 2010 yielded these results: "Whilst, in 1965, 81% of the French declared themselves as Catholics, there were no more than 64% in 2009,"[13] and the diminishing numbers of observant Catholics was significant. "Whilst 27% of the French went to Mass once a week or more in 1952, there are no more than 4.5% in 2006."[14] Additionally, a religion poll from December 2006 found that 32 percent of the French population described themselves as agnostic, a further 32 percent as atheist, and only 27 percent believed in any type of God or supreme being.[15]

It is in this atmosphere that a Jewish teacher gets suspended for teaching "too much" about the Holocaust. Catherine Pederzoli was accused of lacking "reserve, neutrality and secularism" in teaching about the Holocaust.[16]

At one time, Catholicism was the state religion in France; today, a Judeo-Christian mind-set in France has diminished to the point of nonexistence. Of course, we all have heard on the news of the way Islam has infiltrated this secular state and is wreaking havoc there. This inevitable dynamic is one of the core messages I am highlighting in this book.

> We as Americans often make the mistake of interpreting our world through a very, well, *American* lens.

2. Coexistence is not what everyone wants.

I want to offer that, after being raised in America (this melting pot of pluralism and multiculturalism), and after having spent a considerable amount of time in the Middle East (where cultural and religious walls and barriers are as thick as they are high), I am concerned that we as Americans often make the mistake of interpreting our world through a very, well, *American* lens. To assume everyone feels the way we do about civil liberties is a catastrophic mistake.

We tend to think that the rest of the world really *is* like Epcot Center.

It's not.

Unlike the last experience you had at Disney, the reality is that, around our world, horrible—really horrible—things are happening. Slavery is rampant in our world today. The brainwashing of children to become suicide bombers. Honor killings and female genital mutilation in the name of religion. There are horrific things going on in our world today. And they are being carried out not by a few lone individuals, but fostered and even legislated by dehumanizing group thought that controls societies. They are not the exception, but the rule.

The parties coming to the table (Islam, secularism and Judeo-Christianity) have irreconcilable differences. We must realize that what we are dealing with is not a circumstantial issue or even an issue of diplomacy or governmental policy, but an ideological one that runs deep into the soil and roots of people groups around the world.

Nothing could better illustrate the fact that coexistence is not what everyone wants than the way that Palestinian leadership has consistently refused to settle with neighboring Israel despite Israel's endless concessions of land. On the contrary, documented maps used by the Palestinian Authority in children's textbooks show a Middle East *without the nation of Israel*. This propaganda (along with other methods of incitement) underscores the bigoted notion that Palestinian control of the entire region is a valid proposition for the future of the Middle East.[17]

One of the major negotiating points for Israeli officials during the Oslo Accords in 1993 was that the Palestinian Arabs stop all incitement campaigns that generated hatred against Jews and Israel. And we can all remember how quickly those promises were broken! To this day, inciting violence by teaching hatred for Jews and for Israel as a national entity has been orchestrated and developed with great care throughout the Muslim world. Textbooks that equate Jews to "pigs and monkeys" are found throughout the Middle East.

As we can see from disturbing news reports of radical clerics like Anwar al-Awlaki of Yemen calling for the death of Americans,[18] and of those in the Arab world rejoicing over the tragic fires that swept through Northern Israel and calling for the destruction of any Arab who helped Israel in its time of need,[19] those who oppose us are interested in a takeover of power, not in coexistence. We need to recognize the implications of this and admit that coexistence is impossible without a demonstration of all parties to pursue a lifestyle of peace that endures.

3. Coexistence denies a Higher Authority.

If you'll think back to the previous chapter, you will recall that we had an extensive discussion of absolutes—of the meaning of moral absolutes and non-absolutes. In it we looked at the houses of Radical Islam, Militant Secularism and Judeo-Christianity, and I explained how two of these are absolutist value systems, and one is not. I also raised the question of whether the non-absolutists (the militant secularists) will be able to suck others away from their absolutist poles with the promise of a utopian coexistence in which we are all the best of friends.

It is important we understand that a non-absolutist system will always bow down to an absolutist system. An absolutist system is stronger than a non-absolutist system because it has a stronger appeal to us humans due to the way we are designed. We have an insatiable need to believe in something, someone, some force greater than ourselves—one of infinite, eternal, absolute power. Since coexistence is rooted in non-absolutist thought, it denies a Higher Authority, insisting instead that we can make it just fine on our own.

It reminds me of the classic scenario of a couple of small children deciding to cook something delectable for their parents. They shut Mom and Dad out of the kitchen—determined to accomplish on their own the same feat their parents do with such ease three times a day. But in addition to making a mess of everything they touch, they come dangerously close to burning the whole house down by fiddling with heavy equipment (like the oven), which they were never meant to touch.

Additionally, we need the Higher Power of God as an arbitrator, or we will argue over something forever because we are inherently selfish creatures. Any number of parties can coexist with one another under the condition they all abide by the same set of rules, but rarely does this happen. Think for a moment about the conflict between the Palestinians and Israelis. Despite help from intermediary nations, including the much-discussed

Roadmap for Peace, despite repeated negotiations, despite Israel's redoubled efforts of surrendering land and releasing scores of prisoners, the prized goal of peace and coexistence remains elusive. Humanly negotiated coexistence leaves out the most important ingredient: God Himself. We cannot treat eternal conflicts with temporal means and expect them to bear lasting results.

So, coexistence is impossible because it depends on human effort. Just as children create disasters by taking on a role too big for them and refusing to answer to an objective voice of reason, humanists do even worse when they decide to play God. When are we going to concede that some things are just above our pay grade? The point is that coexistence will remain a myth because it does not answer the innate need within people that compels them to search for, believe in and submit to a Higher Authority.

> Any number of parties can coexist with one another under the condition they all abide by the same set of rules.

Land of Liberty

Again, I must refer back to America's inception, which sought to maintain or allow for the connection of people to God without the interference of any system that could insert itself in between. America's founders had witnessed firsthand the lack of freedom that results from a theocratic stranglehold, and so, devised a system of government with not one, not two, but three branches, all kept from exerting too much power through a system of checks and balances. They were smart enough to do this because their biblical worldview taught them that human nature is inherently flawed, and therefore they felt obligated to ensure the citizens of this new world that they would never be subjected to tyranny. The guiding principle here was to keep one individual or ruling authority from asserting too much control, which can so easily come to illegitimately challenge the Highest Authority—God's.

The ways in which some of our politicians today think they can negotiate with totalitarian dictators who are not interested in playing fair, but take any advantage they are given, remind me of Neville Chamberlain's attempts to appease Hitler. (In case you are forgetting, Chamberlain's cowardly strategies did not produce peace, but only put off the inevitable.) Our founding fathers had different means of addressing national and international issues—such as self-sacrifice, courage and prayer.

> In the beginning of the contest with Britain, when we were sensible of danger, we had daily prayers in this room for Divine protection. Our prayers, Sir, were heard, and they were graciously answered. . . . Do we imagine we no longer need His assistance?
>
> —Benjamin Franklin, June 28, 1787,
> to the Constitutional Convention[20]

> It would be peculiarly improper to omit in this first official act my fervent supplications to that Almighty Being who rules over the universe, who presides in the councils of nations, and whose providential aids can supply every human defect.
>
> —George Washington, April 30, 1789,
> in his First Inaugural Address[21]

Like these men, I believe in democracy as an honorable form of earthly government. The ideals of capitalism, private ownership, human rights and freedom of expression have done much to advance the cause of good in America and in other nations of the world. They are appropriate means for conducting civil affairs in a world riddled with sin and imperfection. If our democracy is to prove effective and just, it must remain grounded in the Judeo-Christian value system from which it has sprung. The standard of measure must remain intact in order for the social governance to carry out what is right and good. It is for lack of this that we see the entire world spinning out of control. The issue is one of Lordship and authority. Whom or what will we ultimately recognize as being in charge of our nation and our world?

Of course, I'm not trying to turn the world into America. (And, at the direction things seem to be going in our government and society at large, I should hope not!) Rather, I am using these ideals as a means of showing us how far we have drifted from them. It seems that now, more often than not, we are morally lazy, money-hungry, overgrown adolescents who are more concerned with preserving our own self-interests than we are with preserving what makes this nation great.

What I am trying to do is help us discern which system or worldview most honors the rights of the individual and protects the liberties and freedoms of each person. Whether you personally believe in the Bible or the Torah or believe in Jesus or not, the culture and society that allows for the most elevated honoring of individual freedoms is the one that also accepts the basic constraints imposed by the moral code of the Bible.

It is patently obvious to most thinking people that societies ruled instead by Sharia are archaic in their expression of government and law. Do I believe there are evil, dangerous people within Christianity? Within Judaism? Absolutely. This is not a book about individuals or even micro-movements within people groups. It is, however, a book about getting us to come to terms with the fact that the world is not like Epcot Center. We struggle to accept the idea that there really are bad people who want to do bad things. We struggle to accept the idea that America will not always be America, that the West will not always be the West.

We're talking about humanity's need for a Higher Authority to arbitrate His affairs, and the failure of a godless, amoral coexistence to meet that need. Whether it topples from within, or is crushed from without, coexistence will ultimately fall.

All of this is rather unpleasant. Wouldn't it be easier to slip back into a misinformed haze and believe everything will somehow work itself out? And if not, what am I advocating—intolerance?

No. I am pointing out the undeniable truth that if we continue to allow the values of tolerance and multiculturalism to be hijacked and redefined by those who only wish to do away with them altogether, we are very soon going to find ourselves living under the same conditions our founders came to this country to escape. The well-meaning West has unsuspectingly walked away from the very foundations that gave it strength at its foundation, and now, a man-made, unattainable idealism called coexistence is about to lure us away from any vestige of freedom and genuine tolerance that remains on the earth.

> **Humankind as a whole is headed toward a great divide. An irrevocable split.**

Consider again what C. S. Lewis wrote in *The Great Divorce*:

> We are not living in a world where all roads are radii of a circle and where all, if followed long enough, will therefore draw gradually nearer and finally meet at the centre: rather in a world where every road, after a few miles, forks into two, and each of those into two again, and at each fork you must make a decision. Even on the biological level life is not like a river, but like a tree. It does not move toward unity but away from it.[22]

Humankind as a whole is headed toward a great divide. An irrevocable split. An un-mendable parting of ways. The distorted values of tolerance and multiculturalism are being used by those who would convince us it is possible to coexist in peace forever without God. This is far from reality. The myth of coexistence, like all myths, will one day be relegated to the realm of bedtime fairy tales and childhood fantasies. Only the truth will remain.

6

The House of Radical Islam

id you know our country is at war with Radical Islam? Not that you would have gotten that impression from the evening news. U.S. news agencies have been coerced into using a highly edited vocabulary when speaking about radical Islamic terror. It is political correctness to the max. Journalists are taught not to use words that accurately describe the threat (*jihad, violent extremism, religious dominance, Sharia*), and instead, perpetuate the misconception that we are not battling a clearly defined enemy. This severely distorts public perception of what we are truly up against by presenting us with a counterfactual image of Islam.

On second thought, it may not be strictly correct to say we are at war with Radical Islam. Perhaps a more accurate way of stating it would be, "*Radical Islam* is at war with *us.*" Whether or not we are willing to acknowledge this and defend our liberties remains to be seen. Unfortunately, with the political correctness that has undermined the faith and resolve of a once-great civilization, we are not putting up much of a fight.

A Battle Over Here

Just a decade ago, Radical Islam was not even a blip on most Americans' radar screens. If anyone had heard of it, it was a problem happening somewhere "over there"—far from our school districts, neighborhoods, shopping centers and airports.

On a Sunday morning in August 2001, I was preaching at a church near Niagara Falls, New York, sharing a message with my fellow believers about our need to be salt and light in the world. To preserve all that is good in society and expose all that is not, we would need to be passionate about pursuing God and informed about the current issues assaulting His Kingdom. I cited the hateful rants and ominous threats of large terrorist organizations whose stated intent is to convert or kill everyone who does not submit to Islam. I was doing everything short of lighting myself on fire in an attempt to get through to the congregation that morning, but nothing worked. I might as well have been warning the wind.

> I was doing everything short of lighting myself on fire in an attempt to get through to the congregation.

Less than two weeks later, a pair of jumbo jets filled with passengers and enough aviation fuel to get them across the continent crashed into New York's World Trade Center, killing nearly 2,600 people. Nine-eleven had happened, and the world would never be the same. The pastor from the church I had spoken at contacted me to let me know his congregants were calling in to his office left and right, requesting copies of the sermon "that guest speaker" had delivered just days before.

Today, of course, it is a different story. The continuous threat of attack from an extensive, international Islamic infrastructure is hard to ignore (although that doesn't stop people from trying). But how aware are we of the methods and overall objectives of these forces of extremism? And just how did devout Islam become one of the most powerful ideological forces in our world today?

History of Islam 101

Across the vast Arabian Desert in the seventh century, there was not much indication of a world power that would arise from this desolate land. Far from the lucrative oil market of the 21st century, Islam was formed among some desert tribesmen united by one leader named Muhammad. At the outset, many of Muhammad's teachings were relatively peaceful—as the early writings in the Quran tend to be—showing high regard for the Hebrew prophets and Jesus Christ. But over time this was to change drastically, and the doctrine and culture of Islam, which literally translated means "surrender" or "submission," became characterized by aggression, hostility and intimidation.

Muhammad was born in the city of Mecca on the Arabian Peninsula in approximately A.D. 570. The details and context of his upbringing have been embellished by oral tradition, but it is known that there were several tribal factions vying for status among the Arabian peoples at the time. Raised in the households of his uncles, Muhammad seized several key opportunities to unite those quarreling factions under his leadership.

In general, Muhammad was known for his redoubled efforts to dispel dissensions and disputes among the Arabian tribes, the backdrop for his experience at age forty during the sacred month of Ramadan. It was at this time Muhammad claimed to have had an encounter with an angel of light (afterward said to have been Gabriel). Muhammad's experience, reciting messages in a way that resembled Arabian soothsaying, was the beginning of his declaration of the new authoritative word known as the Quran.[1]

Thought by some to be a magician operating under evil powers, Muhammad nevertheless persisted in preaching his message, which succeeded in bringing an ever-increasing group of followers around him, which faced ongoing attacks from outside.

Because his new teaching of united worship to one god was not accepted by all, Muhammad's followers fled a few times to avoid the persecution, culminating in their significant relocation to the city of Yathrib (later Medina) in 622. This marked a significant event in the early establishment of Islam, and this migration (*hijra*) marks the New Year on the Islamic calendar to this day.[2] We can also identify a turning point in the development of Islam in conjunction with this immigration. It was in Medina that violence against non-Muslims (particularly the Jews) began with vigor, and the words and teachings of Muhammad recorded later in the Quran become very violent in nature. One example is from Sura 9:5, which says, "Then slay the idolaters wherever you find them, and take them captives and besiege them and lie in wait for them in every ambush" (Shakir translation).

Because of the influence gained by Muhammad through fierce tactics of intimidation and warfare, forced conversions to Islam and the appeal to the masses, the house of Islam came to the forefront in world affairs as a dominating caliphate. This term signifies a ruling authority over Muslim lands, as instituted by caliphs (governing leaders), the first of whom were the successors to Muhammad. The presence of this type of Muslim rule could be seen up until the days of the Turkish Ottoman Empire, which was the last of the ruling caliphates that spanned the territory of multiple modern-day nations. Although the Ottoman Empire fell in the early twentieth century, the ideal of a Muslim caliphate persists to the present day among devout Muslims who desire to see the world under Islamic rule.

A Peaceful Religion?

The backbone of Islam both past and present is a belief in the authority of the Quran, the book of holy writings given through the prophet Muhammad. We may view this book as imaginative, innocent or merely cultural like something out of *Arabian Nights,* but religious Muslims take its teachings very seriously and enact them into 21st century life. Amazingly, even the violent practices that would appear to many of us as tribally primitive are taken as legally binding language for implementation in the modern world.

The radical Islamic terrorism we hear about so often is possible because Muslims do not ascribe to the American ideal that religious beliefs should be freely chosen by individuals, and not imposed by the government. As Pastor Stuart Robinson has written in his key book *Mosques and Miracles,* "Islam encompasses the whole spectrum of life—political, public, economic, legal, and social. It will not be relegated to the domain of religious isolation. For Muslims the whole of life is seamlessly, interconnectedly religious."[3]

> Far from being just a religion, Islam is better understood as a political ideology.

Michael Scheuer, former head of the CIA unit that was assigned to track Osama bin Laden, wrote in *Through Our Enemies' Eyes,* "Contemporary Americans . . . are much less conversant and comfortable than contemporary Muslims with religious tenets that shape day-to-day individual and societal behavior and that establish well-defined and fairly inflexible rules for personal behavior, relationships within families and between individuals, and intercourse among nations and religions."[4] Far from being just a religion, Islam is better understood as a political ideology that mobilizes its believers through the authority exercised by its religious leaders.

The Quran itself proves this in many ways. Nonie Darwish, who grew up in an Egyptian family with radical ties and now speaks out against Radical Islam, writes, "There are 146 references to hell in the Quran. Only 6 percent of those in hell are there for moral failings, such as murder or theft. The other 94 percent in hell are for the intellectual sin of disagreeing with Mohammed, a political crime. Hence, Islamic hell is a political prison for those who speak against Islam."[5] It is in this context that legislation like the Muslim blasphemy law comes into play, under which those who face the mere *accusation* of blaspheming the prophet Muhammad are subject to legal death. Clearly, Islam is not just a set of beliefs its followers are urged to ascribe to personally, but a legalistic political regime that is to be brutally enforced on everyone.

At this point you may still be thinking, *Well, that may be how it is in Saudi Arabia, Pakistan or Iran, but not in America, Canada or England! After all, I've heard that Islam is mostly a peaceful religion, especially in the West.* Despite the fact that there are moderate Muslims who see their religion in a different light, and genuinely desire to live peaceably and civilly among others, they seem to be a minority. And sadly, they are often the first ones to fall victim to the sword of Radical Islam.

Islam is no longer a distant, foreign issue that we as Americans or Western Christians can safely ignore. The house of Radical Islam, wherever it operates, is based upon an understanding that the world is divided into only two categories: the house of Islam (*Dar al-Islam*) and the house of war (*Dar al-Harb*). *Dar al-Islam* is wherever Islamic rule has been established, and the remainder of the world is considered *Dar al-Harb,* a field of war in which the opposers must be fought so that their territories can be conquered for Allah. Their end goal of global domination is stark and irrevocable, with no room for negotiation.

We do ourselves a disservice, however, when we think of this Muslim war on the West as being waged only through physical violence. Most of this battle is actually taking place ideologically via information warfare. Their first line of attack is on a much more subtle level than blowing up buildings. If they can control the information we receive and share as well as the language we use to do so, they can control us. This infiltration tactic is known as "soft jihad" or "stealth jihad." This strategic warfare is part of an intricate, phased plan of the Muslim Brotherhood's to enlist the help of Westerners in its mission to demolish our civilization. This multifaceted network of individuals and organizations throughout the world is the primary instrument by which the Islamic global takeover is being implemented. Consider the Muslim Brotherhood's mission statement, taken from a covert document titled "An Explanatory Memorandum on the General Strategic Goal for the Group in North America":

> The Ikhwan [Muslim Brotherhood] must understand that their work in America is a kind of grand Jihad in eliminating and destroying the Western civilization from within and "sabotaging" its miserable house by their hands and the hands of the believers [Muslims] so that it is eliminated and God's religion [Islam] is made victorious over all other religions.[6]

Sounds like a clearly defined enemy to me! Yet the leaders of our nation seem intent on appeasing such radicals who have openly declared their objective of destroying us. Could it be the reason for this lies in the fact that our government agencies have already been infiltrated by Islamists to such a degree we do not have full sovereignty in our own ruling bodies? Everyone knows that the number-one rule in war is to "know your enemy." But how can we conquer an enemy we are not allowed to identify accurately? How can we analyze something we are not permitted to define? How can we fight back against evil forces when we are too afraid to call them for what they are?

The Muslim Brotherhood (a terrorist infrastructure, from which Hamas has sprung) operates through many front organizations in the West. It is the oldest Islamic society, and its credo is, "Allah is our objective. The Prophet is our leader. Qur'an is our law. Jihad is our way. Dying in the way of Allah is our highest hope." Below is a partial listing of entities that some have suggested may be linked to The Muslim Brotherhood:

- Islamic Society of North America
- North American Islamic Trust
- Muslim Students Association
- Muslims for America
- American Muslim Task Force
- Council on American Islamic Relations

The members of these and similar associations are politically active, often wealthy and influential, and have short-term goals and long-term vision for imposing their supremacist theocracy in every sphere. Additionally, the Organisation of The Islamic Conference—the largest international organization other than the United Nations—is poised to exert formal global dominance the minute it gets the chance.

Islamic Holy War

From the days of Muhammad until now, the military component of Islam has been in operation, known according to its religious basis as *jihad*. The word *jihad* encompasses more than one meaning (evidence of the dualistic thinking of Islam, which we will come to in a moment). In many usages, *jihad* refers to an inner struggle of the Muslim to live for Allah, against forces of evil that would thwart this effort. Although Islamic groups often give this definition publicly, the word *jihad* or "struggle" more often refers to armed war and terrorism against the perceived enemies of Islam. Historically this has been carried out first and most viciously against the Jewish people, but it is now undertaken just as vigorously against Christians and other groups that do not accept the rule of Islam.

Islam's war against the other peoples of the world is really a centuries-old battle that began long before Muhammad himself. Genesis 16 records the story of Abraham's son, Ishmael, who was born to his Egyptian maidservant Hagar. Before he was born, the angel of the Lord said, "His hand shall be against every man, and every man's hand against him" (v. 12). The Lord also said of Ishmael, "I will make him a great nation. But My covenant I will establish with Isaac" (Genesis 17:20–21). As history has shown, time after time the descendants of Abraham's line through Ishmael have warred against the line established through Isaac and Jacob (who was renamed Israel). In recent centuries, this onslaught has steadily intensified and has resulted in the volatile, global epidemic of terrorism it is now. Those who have been brought into Islam either through birth or through conversion (often by the sword) have inherited a long-established hatred toward non-Muslims that has been passed down for generations.

> The word *jihad* or "struggle" more often refers to armed war and terrorism.

In this environment of hostility, Islamic clerics have incited their communities to wage an aggressive and multifaceted *jihad* against the non-Muslim "infidels" (*kuffar*) far and wide. Typically only three choices have been given to the infidel (*kafir*) encountering Muslim *jihad*: to pay a heavy tax, known as the *jizya*, to convert to Islam or to suffer death. In many cases only the latter two options have been given, resulting in widespread carnage in Muslim lands. Those who have been able to pay the *jizya* live under Muslim rule and are known as *dhimmis*—second-class citizens who are afforded even worse treatment than others under Muslim rule.

It would be erroneous of us to think that just because a Muslim suicide bomber has not crossed our morning newsfeed we have averted the advances of Radical Islam. You see, soft jihad (also known as political or cultural jihad) works hand in hand with violent, hard jihad. When Islamists are given enough leeway, they work to create isolated enclaves—Muslim state-within-states—that serve as platforms to fuel their religiously motivated aggression. Unbelievably, there are many such enclaves being formed in America today. This trend reflects what is happening in Europe, where the Muslim population is exploding because of high birthrates and immigration. They do not assimilate into society as a whole, but instead live together in urban areas. There is a resultant natural hostility toward outside authority, which makes police afraid to enforce law there. At least 750 "Sensitive Urban Zones," a roundabout way of saying "No Go Zones," have been identified in France. These are regions so dangerous that the government has officially designated them as areas in which they cannot exercise effective control.[7]

> The goal of jihad is to establish Islamic supremacy throughout the world.

Keep in mind: the goal of jihad is to establish Islamic supremacy throughout the world by implementing what is known as Sharia law or Sharia-based governance. Sharia law, practiced in countries like Saudi Arabia and Iran, is known for its grievous violations of human rights, its horrendous treatment of women and its repression of freedoms we take for granted (freedom of the press, freedom of religion and private ownership). Domestic life under Sharia law permits atrocious acts to be perpetrated against those who—either intentionally or unintentionally—disobey it.

Nothing typifies this better and more horrifically than the custom of honor killings in the Muslim world. An "honor killing" is one in which family members brutally murder their own flesh and blood after the person allegedly commits some misdeed that shames their family. While the custom is not exclusive to any single culture or religion, these established ritual murders, prevalent within Islamic societies, have become a hallmark of Islam's terrifying culture.

The United Nations Population Fund (UNFPA) reports that as many as five thousand women and girls every year are murdered by family members for "dishonoring the family."[8] In Islamic nations across the Middle East, Asia, Southeast Asia, North America and Europe, human rights groups and women's rights groups say the figures are even higher because many cases go unreported.

"Honour killings are on the rise worldwide," says Asma Jahangir, United Nations special investigator on extrajudicial, summary and arbitrary executions. Jahangir is also a UN special investigator on violence against women. In 2000 in her annual report to the Commission on Human Rights, Jahangir wrote, "Such killings have been reported in Bangladesh, Brazil, Ecuador, Egypt, India, Gaza and the West Bank [Israel], Italy, Jordan, Morocco, Pakistan, Sweden, Turkey, Uganda and the United Kingdom." Again, while honor killings have been known to take place all over the world, the report states that they tend to be more prevalent in countries with a majority Muslim population.[9] Let's pick one of these countries and zoom in for a closer look.

One report gives chilling detail:

Every year, between 25 and 50 women and girls are the victims of "honour" killings in Jordan. . . . Kifaya, a girl of 12 from Jordan, was reported to have returned home one evening from a walk with some friends. On returning home, her father accosted her with heavy sticks and an iron chain. He beat her to death, shouting that she had dishonored the entire family. He told police he killed his only daughter because she went for walks without his permission. About the same time, a young woman

named Hanan, 34, was shot dead by her brother for the "crime"
of marrying a Christian. Her brother left her body in the street
and smoked a cigarette while he waited for the police to arrive.[10]

As apt as we may be to shudder and turn away, these vicious,
malevolent attacks are not something happening "over there."
They are happening "over here"—right in our own communities. Consider these examples of violent "honor killings" that
have taken place in recent years across the U.S.:

- In 2011, an Iraqi-born Muslim, Faleh Hassan Almaleki,
  was convicted of second-degree murder for the murder of
  his twenty-year-old daughter, Noor, in what was classified
  by a court in Arizona as an "honor killing."[11]
- In 2008, Chaudhry Rashid, a Pakistani-born resident of
  Jonesboro, Georgia, murdered his daughter, Sandeela Kan-
  wal, because she wanted to divorce an older man from
  Pakistan whom Rashid had forced her to marry.[12]
- In Dallas, Texas, in 2008, Sarah Said, seventeen, and her
  eighteen-year-old sister, Amina, were killed on New Year's
  Day by their Egyptian-born father who fled the country after
  the murder. The frantic 9-1-1 call captures their final moments as they lie bleeding to death from gunshot wounds.[13]
- In 2009, Muzzamil "Mo" Hassan, a television executive
  from western New York, murdered his wife, Aasyia, because she had filed for divorce. This case strikes a personal
  chord for me, because it happened not twenty minutes from
  where I live. Just before Valentine's Day, this businessman
  stabbed his estranged wife over forty times and beheaded
  her in the hallway of his television studio. Making this
  painful situation painfully ironic is the fact that Hassan
  was the founder of a local Muslim television network called
  Bridges TV. The network's purpose was to portray Muslims in a more positive light.[14]

Sadly, this is just a sampling of these horrific events. The list could go on and on.

Pillars and Practices

Islam is built upon five pillars of faith that determine religious observance. Upon these rest the power of the ideology that drives the house of Radical Islam. On the surface, they may sound similar in form to the tenets of Judaism and Christianity, but it's not difficult to see how they contrast in function. The five pillars of Islam are as follows.

1. Confession of the creed (shahadah)

At the core of Islam is a simple, authoritative confession that drives all Muslim observance. In its short form, the confession reads, "There is no god but Allah; Muhammad is the Apostle (or prophet / messenger) of Allah." This confession is not simply a matter of private personal faith; it is to be repeated out loud publicly—adding to its strength in the individual in the midst of the Muslim *ummah* (community). The declaration is used both in daily personal religious observance as well as the corporate call to prayer five times a day.[15] It is a statement of unyielding absolutes, directing the worship of its adherents. In this lifestyle of constant credal confession, devout Muslims are known for shouting "*Allahu Akbar*" ("God is great" or "God is greater") when carrying out acts of violence in the name of Allah, which are performed as false worship.

2. Prayers (salat)

Much of the strength of Islam as a house is due to the fact that it functions as a house of prayer. Five times a day, in replication of Muhammad's personal practice, observant Muslims recite their prayers.[16] As they do so, they pray toward Mecca, the location of the mosque where the Kaba is found, which they believe to have been built by Abraham and Ishmael.[17] Prior to each observance of prayers, Muslims must perform a ceremonial washing for self-cleansing. It is my firm belief that the only reason Islam is able to wield so much influence on a global scale is because Muslims take this injunction seriously. By praying as a corporate house of prayer, they invoke supernatural realities into their existence on this earth (more to come on this in chapter 9).

3. Fasting (saum)

Viewed by some as archaic in modern times, fasting is nevertheless an extremely powerful force in Islam to this day. The month-long fast of Ramadan each year serves as a point of unity required for all Muslims and adds an increased element of strictness to the discipline of prayer and fasting observed throughout the year. Having said this, in cultural practice there is quite a bit of leniency after twilight, when Muslims are typically permitted to eat, drink and even party. Because observant Muslims during this time of fasting are more intently focused upon prayer, study of the Quran and corporate participation, the collective impact upon the entire community is multiplied. Regrettably, this often means that religious violence and incitement are the fruits of the Ramadan fast.

4. Giving of alms (zakat)

In Islam, the zakat is an obligatory payment to charity, approximately 2.5 percent of each believer's yearly income. This contribution, in practice essentially a tax, is used to help such people as the needy and infirm, but is also used for the overall spread of Islam.[18] In contrast to other religions, the zakat can only be directed to other Muslims, not to the needy in the world in general. Important to note is the fact that an eligible use of the zakat is to fund those who are engaged in voluntary jihad

(Muslim holy war). This last point has enormous implications to the funding of terrorism against non-Muslims, who according to Islam are part of the *Dar al-Harb* (house of war).

5. Pilgrimage to Mecca (hajj)

Every Muslim is required to make at least one pilgrimage (*hajj*) to Mecca, the holiest city in Islam, located in modern-day Saudi Arabia. In accepted practice, notable exceptions are made for those who are unable to make the trip, though the pilgrimage (which occurs yearly in the twelfth Islamic month) is still deemed a fundamental part of salvation.[19] The hajj and the city of Mecca in general are completely closed to non-Muslims, who are not permitted to enter at any time. (Can you imagine the public outcry if the Jewish people were to make Jerusalem off-limits to Gentiles?) Because of the value placed on this aspect of Islam, many Muslim believers make multiple pilgrimages in their lifetime. As they visit the Kaba, elements of the hajj ceremonies include animal sacrifice, shaving of the heads of the pilgrims, circumambulations around the Kaba and even self-flagellation.

The complex nature of Islam stems from the fact that Islam is not simply a religion, but a system of rule. "Radical Islam," in this sense, is actually a redundant phrase because those who actually live by the dictates of the Quran and the teachings of Muhammad are, by modern definition, radical. While it's true there are many peaceful Muslims, this is only because they are either giving a false appearance of benevolence or they are genuinely not embracing the full teaching of Islam, but instead are attempting to redefine their faith from within it.

Radical Islam is the dominant force within Islam, and it will never peacefully coexist with the non-Muslim world or with Muslims of different beliefs. All radical Muslims believe in fighting until their version of Islam conquers the world. Though they may differ on what is permissible in achieving this end,

111

the ultimate goal is the same: a world full of Muslims and no one else.

A Dangerous Misunderstanding

Where the West has perhaps most categorically misunderstood Radical Islam is the fact that this ideology does not play by the same rules they do. Because the ultimate goal of Islam is unequivocally to rule the world, it is not considered sinful to lie, kill or use deception or terrorism to accomplish this end.

Unlike the Bible and other religious works, the Quran is written under the premise that later "revelations" supersede prior ones. Thus in Islam, inherent contradictions are not problematic because of the progressive authority given to the later works and sayings of Muhammad. Since the later revelations have been given the authority to change or even reverse prior revelations, early benign passages of the Quran do not have an upper hand against later violent portions like the Sura of Muhammad mentioned above.

Along with the Quran, the Hadith (supplemental writings about the life and teachings of Muhammad) give further authoritative instruction to devout Muslims concerning the way of life passed down by Muhammad. Equally violent in nature, the Hadith contain incendiary sayings of Muhammad such as, "The Hour [Day of Resurrection] will not arrive until you fight the Jews, [literally, until a Jew will hide behind a rock or tree] and the rock and the tree will say: Oh Muslim, servant of Allah, there is a Jew behind me, come and kill him!"[20] Thus these violent, extremist tendencies are integral to those who seek to wholeheartedly live by Muhammad's teachings as found in the Quran and Hadith.

Here is where we come to a critical concept in the house of Islam, known as *dualism*. Bill Warner, the director of the Center for the Study of Political Islam, asserts that "dualism is the foundation and key to understanding Islam."[21] Simply put, dualism is the belief that two contradictory realities can operate simultaneously and both be true. Thus the earlier peaceful writings of the Quran, though superseded by the later more violent writings, can still be used and declared legitimate. In the political agenda of Islam, this conflicting logic is commonly used in the rhetoric of those who declare that Islam is a religion of peace.

In similar fashion, the concept known as *taqiyya*, meaning the Quran gives permission to Muslims to lie in order to advance the faith or Allah's cause, is a distinguishing mark of this paradigm. Others would call this deceitful. But because of the convenient disregard of personal integrity, a Muslim leader can still be faithful to Islam by lying publicly to those outside in order to advance the cause of totalitarianism. By these methods, Islam is able to infiltrate new territory by appearing peaceful but simultaneously communicating in incendiary ways among fellow Muslims.

> Islam is able to infiltrate new territory by appearing peaceful.

To see this principle in action, simply look at the life of the late Yasser Arafat, chairman of the Palestine Liberation Organization (PLO) and president of the Palestinian Authority (PA). After Arafat agreed with Israeli Prime Minister Yitzhak Rabin on the Oslo Peace Process in 1993, pledging the end of Palestinian violence against Israel and calls for Israel's destruction, Arafat later spoke to Arabs using rhetoric such as this speech in 1996: "You understand that we plan to eliminate the State of Israel and establish a purely Palestinian State. We will make life unbearable for Jews by psychological warfare and population explosion."[22] When speaking to Arabs, Arafat continued to promote jihad (Islamic holy war), while giving an entirely different message to the rest of the world.

Radical Islam is invading not only Islam in general and becoming normative in many locations worldwide; it is also invading Western culture—seeking to subjugate it, destroy it, even replace it. In mosques around the world, America is proclaimed as the "Great Satan" and Israel as the "Little Satan," and outright war has been declared against us both. In a day when suicide bombers are celebrated by their families for their acts of so-called heroism, we must understand that a battle between houses is taking place. Radical Islam shows no signs of backing down. If we do not confront this reality, our lack of confrontation will simply confirm it through silence. At all times, we must speak the truth in love (see Ephesians 4:15) about every aspect of every culture.

7

The House of Militant Secularism

For those of us living in the post-Christian West, the dominant culture of our day is secularism. To be effective within this context, we must be able to see it accurately.

What are the features of secularism?

What is its legacy?

How does it operate and what level of influence does it hold in our institutions?

These are the questions we will be answering in this chapter. Let's begin by considering a quote from one of religion's most infamous naysayers.

Prominent atheist poster boy Richard Dawkins made waves when his 2006 bestseller *The God Delusion* hit bookstores. His book, which came out at the same time as several other similarly hostile titles, highlighted the increasing intensity with which the secular agenda is seeking to aggressively destroy any possibility of theistic creationism at any level. So he argues,

> The God of the Old Testament is arguably the most unpleasant character in all fiction: jealous and proud of it; a petty, unjust, unforgiving control-freak; a vindictive, bloodthirsty ethnic cleanser; a misogynistic, homophobic, racist, infanticidal, genocidal, filicidal, pestilential, megalomaniacal, sadomasochistic, capriciously malevolent bully.[1]

Although many rightly dismiss Dawkins as an angry, ill-informed and, well, *deluded* pseudoscientist, he nevertheless is telling the unregenerate public exactly what they want to hear, and so, is regarded as a man of staggering intellect.

It would be most untrue, however, to conclude that all atheists' affronts to a theistic worldview are so blatant. In fact, most are anything but. So if you have never met someone who introduced himself or herself as a secular humanist, you are not alone. Just because you've never heard of the American Humanist Association (headquartered in Washington, D.C., by the way) and cannot name who won the "Humanist of the Year" award for 2010 (it was Bill Nye the Science Guy!) does not mean secular humanism doesn't profoundly affect every aspect of your daily life. There is a much more subtle (but no less militant) version of secularism permeating Western culture that equally seeks to undermine the monotheism and resultant moral principles that have long served as the bedrock of our society.

It could be argued that many within the secular milieu would define themselves as "seekers" or state outright that they do not know what they believe. This does not mean, however, that their culture, in many ways more amorphous than other schools of thought, is not a monolithic force operating in an intentional way.

Secular humanism is everywhere; it is the most established school of thought currently shaping prevailing culture. The secular world, in which we do most of our living, working, breathing and dying is, in fact, an organism fueled by humanist beliefs and values. Education, the art world, network television

116

and multiple other cultural forces are the tools used to construct this house of thought. Humanists such as Tina Fey, Bill Maher, Carl Sagan, John Lennon and Ricky Gervais are just a few of the household names who have and are influencing popular culture in monumental ways. Their theories are in your kids' textbooks, their music blares through the department stores you shop in and their jokes and rants monopolize the airwaves in your living room most nights of the week.

> Secular humanism is everywhere; it is the most established school of thought currently shaping prevailing culture.

Through both overt and covert means, the art, scholarship and commentary these culture-shapers have exerted on society have served to discredit faith. Their efforts are usually directed at undermining traditional faith in the God of the Bible. They operate through displays of mockery, contempt, condescension and subversion. And, yes, they *do* want your children.

Humanism's Proud Beginnings

Today's typical humanist, whom you will encounter at a family reunion or in an office cubicle, will most likely describe him or herself as someone who has no religion. When the humanist agenda first began to infiltrate the public sphere in America, however, there was no attempt to keep its religious nature a secret.

Progressivism sought to reform the nation on many levels, and philosophers like John Dewey wielded immense influence by forever altering our societal fabric. Dewey even referred to humanism as *A Common Faith* in his work of the same title, which advocated for an ecumenical belief system based in humanistic values compatible with his views of ethics and biology.[2]

His mission was to create a pluralistic moral code, palatable to all mankind, which he theorized would allow humanity to continue to progress in its evolutionary destiny, without experiencing any negative side effects along the way.

Dewey's contemporary and fellow humanist Charles Francis Potter, who authored a similarly-themed book, *Humanism: A New Religion,* blatantly stated the movement's objective to supplant a theistic religion with an atheistic one.

> Education is the most powerful ally of Humanism, and every American public school is a school of Humanism. What can the theistic Sunday schools, meeting for an hour once a week, and teaching only a fraction of the children, do to stem the tide of a five-day program of humanistic teaching.[3]

As we can clearly see, Dewey and his counterparts openly and proudly identified humanism as a kind of religion—even a faith—and others understood this to be unequivocally the case. From obtaining tax-exempt status as a religious organization in the 1950s to being acknowledged as such by the U.S. Supreme Court shortly thereafter, humanism's religious status is a matter of public record.

After several decades, however, the humanists began to back-pedal when their religious status threatened their quest to proselytize their secular dogma. If secular humanism were a religion, why should it be allowed to be propagated through the public school system when Christianity and other religions had been expelled? Quite obviously, it should not, which is why efforts needed to be made to create a strategic duality in the way humanism was to be presented in the public realm. The process ensued by which this self-proclaimed "new religion" shifted from overt to covert tactics, aided by secularist courts, long since dominated by humanist thought. The key was to do some fancy footwork jumping back and forth between the establishment clause and the free exercise clause of the First Amendment.

The rulings, conveniently, allowed humanism to undergo a chameleon-like change between religious and non-religious status, depending on whether or not being termed a religion benefited it at the moment. In short, this means that humanism has grown and flourished in this nation, enjoying all the benefits of a traditional religion, without experiencing any of the restraints placed upon conventional faiths.

> **Humanism is taught to tens of millions of Americans through the public school system (and has been for decades) with complete freedom and exclusivity.**

The end result is that humanism is taught to tens of millions of Americans through the public school system (and has been for decades) with complete freedom and exclusivity. It is no wonder that these values have so permeated every facet of society to the end that we have become unconscious of them. This is, of course, the very essence of religious culture—that the adherents of a particular culture take its fundamental beliefs to be self-evident; that being whatever-it-is-one-is seems the only way to be.

Since the days of Dewey, secularists have been working feverishly to expunge any and all traces of God from society, as these two exasperating cases illustrate:

- In 2010, executives of one of Europe's largest shopping malls blocked the "Hallelujah Chorus"—traditionally associated with Christmastime—from being sung among their shoppers. In Sheffield, South Yorkshire, England, the executives of the Meadowhall shopping center, citing religious "impartiality," refused to allow a brief surprise choir performance of the song among the public (a popular "flash mob"), a style that has met with tremendous positive reception elsewhere in the world, such as Canada.[4]

- A University of Illinois instructor was fired—remember, this is in America—simply because he held Catholic beliefs. Not only that, but he was fired for teaching Catholic beliefs in a class on . . . get this . . . Catholicism![5]

While education is the vehicle with which secularists communicate their creed, materialism is the currency that propels it throughout the culture.

The "Heart" of Secularism

When you hear the word *materialism* what images come to mind? A luxury car? A closet full of designer clothes? A shopping mall? To most of us, the thought of being materialistic would be synonymous with being shallow, phony, superficial . . . not noble qualities, but at the same time, probably not the worst things that one can be. Who of us hasn't made a New Year's resolution to spend less and be more content to live within our means? While not allowing worldly riches to gain an unhealthy hold in our lives, it is important to make a distinction between a materialistic person and a materialistic worldview.

A materialistic person is the one we have just described— someone who has let "stuff" become more important to him or her than anything else. A materialistic worldview, by contrast, is one in which a material reality is the only reality there is. It's bad enough when an individual does it, but when people collectively set standards and define worth based solely on what they can see or touch or buy or sell, the effects are exponentially worse.

A Material World

I'm sure there is precious little in this life that pop icon Madonna and I could agree on besides the fact that we are, thanks to sinful nature, creatures driven by our senses, and living in a material world. The vast excess of material objects that populate the lives of the wealthy Western world are the first pieces of evidence. Did you know that, if you were in the market for them, you could spend more than $1,200 on a pair of blue jeans? $1,200. Really? *They're just jeans!* They will wear out—tear—fade. They will not outlast us. And even if they *do* outlast us—what good will they ultimately do us? None.

If, however, there is no afterlife—no ultimate state of reward that can be sown into now by dying to our temporal desires— what point would there be to our existence other than to make all we can . . . and spend it? In terms of the individual, the blue jeans scenario seems tragic, yes, but basically harmless. It is when we think of materialism in universal terms that we are able to see how detrimental it truly is.

This tenet of materialism is also known as Naturalism—a philosophical concept characteristic of the secular humanist worldview. Naturalism is the opposite of supernaturalism. It asserts that nothing exists that cannot be measured or observed objectively. In such a world, there is no God, nor is there a human spirit. We are merely sophisticated machines that happen to look different from laptops.

Variants of this concept, such as Dialectical Materialism (a Marxist-Leninist theory), take materialism to the extreme. In it, humanity itself loses any intrinsic value it might have had, and is swallowed up into a collective unit, erasing any sense of individuality or created worth. The progenitors of this philosophy took materialism to the max, reasoning that if our existence is entirely comprised of matter alone, our only purpose is to produce more matter.

On a related note, the maxim *Arbeit Macht Frei* (translated "Work will make you free"), which greeted prisoners as they arrived at Nazi concentration camps, is part of the twisted legacy of these fascist anti-Semites. As the Nazis annihilated some six million Jews and other innocent minorities during the Second World War, they believed they were allowing this "subhuman race" to "correct" what was wrong with it. In other words, "Being a productive member of society (by producing more matter) will redeem you from being the plague on society that you are."

The ultimate extreme of humanism is that no personal qualities, emotions or desires are to be valued—only productivity. To achieve this end, people would need to be incorporated into a mass social structure (e.g., a nation-state) to achieve their maximum effectiveness as producers of more of what they are: matter. The social structure of such a nation-state was considered (and still is by many) to be the ultimate level humanity can evolve into.

This belief is widely regarded as the ultimate negation of a created order with inherent value and relational purpose. We do not need to look to this extreme to witness the effects of a society that denies true meaning in favor of productivity. Regular, everyday people with jobs and kids and hopes and car payments are stuck in a heartbreaking downward spiral of emptiness and futility. From new gadgets to morning talk shows, we are inundated with theories about what happiness is and how we can achieve it. Our lives become an attempt to chase down this elusive state of fulfillment instead of what they were meant to be.

It would be narrow of us, of course, to assume that we have a corner on this kind of angst. Despair is a universal trait of every culture that is cut off from its Life source, which at once satisfies our inner longings and impels us to live for higher ends.

Consider these words from Solomon, one of history's wealthiest rulers ever, who demonstrates the truism that wealth does not make us happy.

> The words of the Preacher, the son of David, king in
> Jerusalem.
> "Vanity of vanities," says the Preacher;
> "Vanity of vanities, all *is* vanity."
> What profit has a man from all his labor
> In which he toils under the sun?

122

> *One* generation passes away, and *another* generation
> comes;
> But the earth abides forever.
> The sun also rises, and the sun goes down,
> And hastens to the place where it arose.
> The wind goes toward the south,
> And turns around to the north;
> The wind whirls about continually,
> And comes again on its circuit.
> All the rivers run into the sea,
> Yet the sea *is* not full;
> To the place from which the rivers come,
> There they return again.
> All things *are* full of labor;
> Man cannot express *it*.
> The eye is not satisfied with seeing,
> Nor the ear filled with hearing.
> That which has been *is* what will be,
> That which *is* done is what will be done,
> And *there is* nothing new under the sun.
>
> Ecclesiastes 1:1–9 (emphasis added)

These timeless words are as easy for mankind to identify with today as they were centuries ago. Whether in Solomon's era or on Main Street, U.S.A., the rejection of God leaves us with a world of objects.

Notice I said "objects," not "people." It would be reasonable to conclude that, "The rejection of God leaves you with a world of people," but people are relational beings created in the image of their Maker, and with Him out of the picture, people are no longer what they were. They are still human in the most rudimentary sense of the word, but they have no inherent identity, and as a result, they have no value other than the one they give themselves, or are assigned by their fellow human beings.

> **The rejection of God leaves us with a world of objects.**

123

This inventing of ourselves and our world using no innate sense of purpose or authority is meant to be a fulfilling, freeing experience. It's like having Mom and Dad away on vacation and the teenage offspring throwing a huge party for all their friends with alcohol and drugs to just have a good time and see what happens. *"What could possibly go wrong?!"*

In short, everything. And everything *has* gone wrong in the humanist experiment. We have just come to the end of what historians and intellectuals are calling "the bloodiest of all centuries." And, as you may be guessing, we owe this bloodbath to the very humanistic philosophies that claim they can right all wrongs.

Humanism's Track Record

If you were to ask the atheist, erudite elite of our day where evil comes from, many would claim that belief in God is the root of all evil and that religiously motivated violence has contributed to most warfare throughout the ages. While religion has, tragically, served as a tool to propagate aggressive and wicked agendas on all too many occasions, it is far from being the cause of most of the bloodshed the world has seen.

A closer look confirms the opposite to be true. It has been the humanistic ideologies of our "advanced, enlightened, liberal" existence that have proved to be the most brutal, malevolent and certainly the most fatal. Again, it's when people decide to edit God out of the picture and erect systems contrary to His character and the natural order He has created that things begin to get very ugly.

The two most notable and most recent evils to be spawned through such agnostic concepts are Fascism and Communism. Most scholars agree that Communism—that seemingly benign philosophy that many perceive as simply a means to ensure everyone is treated fairly and that everyone has enough—has alone wiped out more than one hundred million people, more than any other ruling party in all of history. And considering the fact that it has been in existence for fewer than a hundred years, that is not a very good track record.

Soviet Communist Party leader Joseph Stalin can lay claim to the unique legacy of killing more than three times the number of people Hitler murdered during his horrific reign. Among these were the many Ukrainians stamped out by militant forces as they tried to resist the movement taking over their farms, livelihoods and cultural identity. In the winter of 1932–33, having had their food supplies stolen and means of transportation thwarted, the people of Ukraine were dying at a rate of 25,000 per day. Those not killed by the bitter cold and malnourishment were taken care of with Soviet bullets. Of the approximately seven million Ukrainians who died in the famine brutally utilized by Stalin's regime, nearly half were children.[6]

Reputable sources estimate the death toll in twentieth-century China to be as high as forty million, attributed directly to Mao Tse-Tung's "Great Leap Forward."[7] In blithe denial that the mass starvation of his own people was of any consequence, the dictator continued to export millions of tons of grain to his Communist counterparts in Eastern Europe. This political move ensured armament of and collusion with his dubious policies.

Philosopher Karl Marx, the Father of Communism himself, whose economic, political and social theories are thought of as the most influential of any from the nineteenth and twentieth centuries, is quoted as saying, "The first requisite for the happiness of the people is the abolition of religion."[8] (It seems not only that time has proved this statement false, but that it has actually proved the opposite true.) There are, however, even more disturbing things to learn about this influential thinker by peering in a little closer.

It is universally accepted that Marx abandoned his Christian upbringing in favor of atheism at an early age, but many question whether Marx was actually, at his core, a Satanist. His

125

writings—including poetry and dramatic texts—often speak of being overtaken by the dark forces of hell and of the pleasure of luring others into an abyss which, while awful, is at least free from the presence of God. Lines such as "My soul, once true to God, is chosen for hell,"[9] and, "I wish to avenge myself against the One who rules above,"[10] color Marx's actions in a more sinister light. He wrote of the desire to feel equal to his Creator—of establishing a rulership that surpassed all others. In a poem addressing humanity, Marx writes, "You will sink down and I shall follow laughing, Whispering in your ears, 'Descend, come with me, friend.'"[11]

It doesn't seem too much to say that Karl Marx was more intent on damning the world than on bettering it. A letter written to him from his father clearly communicates a sense of concern that his son was being demonically influenced.[12] Although it is not clear why this young German man with a sharp mind and promising future would have had reason to develop philosophies so obviously based in despair, it is undeniable that Karl Marx succumbed to whatever dark force was fueling his ideology.

I believe this can account for much of the turmoil of our 21st-century world, in which as many as one-third of the inhabitants could be considered, on some level, Marxists. It also comes as no surprise to me that the largest atheistic movement in all of history is rooted not in ambivalence of God, but in animosity toward Him.

No One Here but Us Humans

Separated from our Creator, we are simultaneously separated from our created purpose. We become hollow automatons, acting out the motions of life, while void of life itself. But because we crave a sense of purpose—a need to believe our existence is not arbitrary—we cannot help but look for it in our surroundings—in the content that makes up our lives.

Feeling such emptiness inside, we reason that the answers must have something to do with what lies outside of us, so we end up looking to our surroundings to find them. But our gaze outward only reflects off the surface of whatever hollow things we look to, and we are left staring back at our own empty selves—the very ones we were trying to get away from in the first place.

Now, the cycle of pain and longing grows more vicious. Without acknowledging God's supremacy, there is no lasting, gratifying meaning within ourselves, so we look again to others, to our actions, to things in hopes that something will mirror back to us the deep longings and unidentifiable imprint engraved onto our souls.

Because we cannot find meaning in anything but the One who gave it to us, when we fail to receive what we need from our environs, we are filled with despair. We are driven to search farther and farther—different cities, different partners, different paths—hoping that one will lead us to the elusive "other" we are looking for.

The writer of Romans addressed this very phenomenon, which occurs whenever people reject God.

For since the creation of the world God's invisible qualities—his eternal power and divine nature—have been clearly seen, being understood from what has been made, so that people are without excuse.

For although they knew God, they neither glorified him as God nor gave thanks to him, but their thinking became futile and their foolish hearts were darkened. Although they claimed to be wise, they became fools and exchanged the glory of the immortal God for images made to look like a mortal human being and birds and animals and reptiles.

Romans 1:20–23, NIV

If we abandon this quest to find meaning and self-worth in others or in things and direct our desires back onto ourselves, we find them distorted, mangled ghosts of what they once were. Any kind of perversion—however contrary to human nature—becomes possible. Accepted. Commonplace. Even encouraged. Everything becomes permissible in the name of self-expression or self-discovery. Initially, there may have been some modest effort to demonstrate restraint, but eventually we had to pull out all the stops so as not to inadvertently miss what we are looking for.

Continuing on from where we left off in the first chapter of Romans, we find these dynamics are precisely the types of issues being discussed:

> Therefore God gave them over in the sinful desires of their hearts to sexual impurity for the degrading of their bodies with one another. They exchanged the truth about God for a lie, and worshiped and served created things rather than the Creator—who is forever praised. Amen.
>
> Because of this, God gave them over to shameful lusts. Even their women exchanged natural sexual relations for unnatural ones. In the same way the men also abandoned natural relations with women and were inflamed with lust for one another. Men committed shameful acts with other men, and received in themselves the due penalty for their error.
>
> Furthermore, just as they did not think it worthwhile to retain the knowledge of God, so God gave them over to a depraved mind, so that they do what ought not to be done. They have become filled with every kind of wickedness, evil, greed and depravity. They are full of envy, murder, strife, deceit and malice. They are gossips, slanderers, God-haters, insolent, arrogant and boastful; they invent ways of doing evil; they disobey their parents; they have no understanding, no fidelity, no love, no mercy.
>
> Romans 1:24–31, NIV

If this was true in the first century, how much more is it true in the 21st century?

The more we push the natural boundaries of our created design, the more distant we grow from the Presence of a God who is good. Eventually, we find ourselves in the hinterlands of the human psyche; and the farther we wander, the darker it becomes.

It's not difficult to see the irony in a system of thought called humanism that succeeds in so degrading humanity. Thus, the paradox of humanism. Again, separated from their Creator, people are no longer able to interact as creations and become objects of a sort themselves.

Interchangeable.

Utilitarian.

Disposable.

How ironic that the very qualities that set us apart as human beings—ingenuity, determination, unity—once disconnected from their source, make us inhumane. Freedom from a higher power—the very thing we hope will allow us to live as we wish—becomes the very thing that destroys us and one another.

> It's not difficult to see the irony in a system of thought called humanism that succeeds in so degrading humanity.

This trend, however, is not deterring secularists from their militant quest to take over the world. Their latest theory as to why their methods are failing is that not enough people are joining in. "How can we be free while there are still so many closed-minded people intent on clinging to their backward thinking and dangerous assertions that there is only one way?"

Their answer to the dilemma of the failed humanist experiment is more of the same. More regulation. More taxation. More control. And this time, on a global scale. Their answer to the dilemma of the failed humanist experiment is globalization.

It's a Meaningless Life

Most of us are familiar with Frank Capra's ode to small-town America, *It's a Wonderful Life,* in which George Bailey (Jimmy Stewart's character) longs to "shake the dust of this crummy little town off my feet and . . . *see the world!*"[13]

Although plenty of young adults still aspire to backpack through Europe, in 1946, when the Capra movie was made, international travel required a lot more than a credit card, a Zagat guide, and a paperless ticket purchased from a laptop. Kids today grow up seeing the world from the time they can turn on Sesame Street. Movies, YouTube and that modern-day version of the neighborhood corner store called Facebook quickly create a universal frame of reference and context for global mobility. It's not surprising for a twentysomething to log in, check her old college roommate's Facebook status and find that she has spontaneously decided to move from Indianapolis to Dubai.

Globalization, that transnational circulation of languages, ideas and information, is not, in and of itself, inherently evil. Globalization can be used for good, and it is in many cases. It is, theoretically, a neutral phenomenon—only dangerous in the wrong hands.

Like Big Brother.

Think about it: In a surveillance society, cameras are installed, tracking devices are implemented and codes are put into place in an effort to protect the innocent and punish the guilty. Of course, the definitions of "innocent" and "guilty" are decided by those in power, so the very measures being enacted could just as easily be used for harm rather than good.

Secular humanist naïveté, which does not believe in black-and-white terms like "good" and "evil," is forging full steam ahead in creating a global utopia. What they do not admit to themselves is that human nature, when left to its own devices, will always gravitate toward evil. In spite of our best intentions and most sincere efforts, when we leave God out of the

130

equation, we cannot help but do wrong. This is because our only good comes from yielding our will to that of a good and loving Creator, who in turn blesses and sanctifies our lives. But without Him, the bad guy will eventually end up winning the election because he rigs it; the poor will always be among us because people are inherently selfish; and globalization will inevitably go sour because people are always striving to be, but never becoming, gods.

Shaking its fist in the face of God, militant secular humanism fails to reach its goal of becoming like God—the temptation that led to humanity's fall in Genesis 3. It represents the ultimate destiny of those eating of the Tree of Knowledge of Good and Evil—knowing and teaching what is good for humanity without the power to actually do what is good; continually researching and documenting the evils of humanity (like global warming, poverty, illiteracy, overpopulation, disease and genocide) without any real ability to remedy these woes. That is because all the problems that plague our world gain their authority from the power of sin and death. So, if one is not willing to acknowledge there is such a thing as evil, one will never be able to wield the restorative power of a good God.

The house of Militant Secularism looks incredibly appealing on the outside, which is why people are flocking to it in droves. But style is never substance, and appearances are certainly deceiving. Is there a house on the block that humanity can actually live in, where it can find true hope and fulfillment? It's time to get beyond the facades of the first two houses in search of prime real estate. Let us turn the corner, shouting, "Move that bus!", as coined by *Extreme Home Makeover,* and the house that can truly be a home will come into view.

8

The House of Judeo-Christianity

After considering the legacies Radical Islam and Militant Secularism have left to the world, we come to consider what the Judeo-Christian worldview offers. In a way, this task may prove to be both easier and more difficult. On one hand, we may be well versed in our own history and worldview, but on the other, it is often hard to secure a proper perspective on something we are so immersed in. Nevertheless, we are left to grapple with the implications of this often very misunderstood worldview, and decide how we (as those who are presumably a part of it) will define it for generations to come.

Nearly forty years ago, Dr. Francis Schaeffer wrote a masterpiece entitled *How Should We Then Live? The Rise and Decline of Western Thought and Culture.*[1] Through Dr. Schaeffer and others like him, the Western world has further awakened to our call to declare truth unashamedly—not just in our own prayer closets, but also in the midst of society itself, where too often we have departed from a foundational commitment to absolutes and the Word of God. The question posed by Schaeffer, "How should we then live?" should motivate us to step fully into our God-given authority as believers in Him.

The God we serve is the God of Abraham, Isaac and Jacob. He has revealed Himself principally through the written Word of the Bible, and also through many other means such as His vast creation, His acts and miracles in

> We can answer the call from God to serve others, steward His creation and be His representatives in the earth.

individual human lives and His intervention in global affairs. From the days of Abraham our father of faith (see Galatians 3:6–9), God has been looking for a people who heed His voice and obey His commands. As Christians, we believe that, through personal and corporate faith, we can answer the call from God to serve others, steward His creation and be His representatives in the earth.

First Things First

To say the Judeo-Christian ethos is an absolutist worldview is an understatement. We pretty much wrote the book on it. (Well, *God* did, to be exact.) The God of the Old and New Testaments minces no words and makes no mistakes in presenting Himself to humanity as the one, true, omnipotent, omnipresent, ever-living God.

> For the LORD is the great God,
> And the great King above all gods.
> In His hand are the deep places of the earth;
> The heights of the hills are His also.
> Psalm 95:3–4

Jesus further declared: "I am the way, the truth, and the life. No one comes to the Father except through Me" (John 14:6).

The name God gives Himself (when He introduces Himself to Moses after four hundred years of silence brought on by His people's rebellion) is "I AM" (see Exodus 3:14). This audacious statement sets God apart as the uncreated progenitor of all existence—the one who doesn't need to give an explanation for who and what He is. Going back even further to God's first interface with the man who was to become Abraham, we find that this larger-than-life God is actually knowable, and is eager to lovingly relate to His creation.

In his masterful exploration of the foundation the Jewish people laid for Western civilization, *The Gifts of the Jews: How a Tribe of Desert Nomads Changed the Way Everyone Thinks and Feels,* Thomas Cahill states that the Jews actually originated the concept of individual identity that has been so absorbed into our contemporary consciousness that we could not exist as we do today without it. The ancient Jews were the first people to see time differently—not as a static cycle of life and death spinning perpetually with no hope of being altered, but as a linear journey in which a better tomorrow could be pursued by courageously following an Unseen Voice by something that would come to be known as *faith*.[2]

Law and Order

After Abraham, God's dealings with humanity became more defined in His interactions with Moses and the Israelites. Having made a promise to Abraham that, through his family line, all families of the earth would be blessed (see Genesis 12:3), He then specified that promise through Moses. How would the nations of the earth be blessed? By walking in accordance with certain guidelines He set in place to govern His people—a way of life that would bring *blessing* to individuals, families, cities and nations.

God gave His inspired truth in written form, which through the centuries has been meticulously preserved and copied in canonical form as the Bible, the most remarkable and influential book ever. True Christians believe the Bible to be the exact, inspired Word of God: "All Scripture is given by inspiration of God, and is profitable for doctrine, for reproof, for correction, for instruction in righteousness" (2 Timothy 3:16), for "men of God spoke as they were moved by the Holy Spirit" (2 Peter 1:21).

The Ten Commandments, chiseled by the finger of God on tablets of stone in the presence of Moses, formed a bedrock for human society to build upon in righteousness, truth and justice. This simple, unadorned ten-line Decalogue has become the foundation for how we, thousands of years later, think, reason and interact with our neighbors every day of our lives.

"You shall have no other gods before Me.

"You shall not make for yourself a carved image—any likeness of anything that is in heaven above, or that is in the earth beneath, or that is in the water under the earth; you shall not bow down to them nor serve them . . .

"You shall not take the name of the LORD your God in vain . . .

"Remember the Sabbath day, to keep it holy . . .

"Honor your father and your mother, that your days may be long upon the land which the LORD your God is giving you.

"You shall not murder.

"You shall not commit adultery.

"You shall not steal.

"You shall not bear false witness against your neighbor.

"You shall not covet."

Exodus 20:3–17

The overarching theme is that God—yes, amazingly, *God,* the all-mighty, all-powerful, all-glorious Creator of heaven and earth—cares about the commonplace events in the lives of all mankind. He cares so much that He set in place a specific moral structure that would guide our daily lives and bring order to our rest, work and worship. By putting His infinite wisdom into simple words we could understand, God came down to our level and got involved with the minutiae of the everyday human experience. He did not just randomly assign some rules to mediate the squabbles of fallen humanity; His commands carried a commitment to uphold the best for each person, as a Father would for His children. Because God created humanity, He knew what was best for us and wove those pieces of knowledge into the fabric of our earthen experience.

His commands carried a commitment to uphold the best for each person.

In his remarkable book *Mere Christianity*,[3] C. S. Lewis has described in brilliant prose the link between the way God has made us (with an inner awareness of moral law) and the system of values and conduct He gave us (guiding outward behavior). God's directives are not arbitrary, but are instead a precise reflection of His infinite understanding as Creator. Because God is a God of order, He has created an intricate reciprocity between human beings, which causes us to fit together hand in glove, and which, if followed, yields the maximum amount of joy and satisfaction we can experience in this life.

When God commands us to live as equals by treating others fairly, He is not introducing an idea foreign to our nature. Quite the opposite: He has already created us to inwardly desire the justice He commands us to live by. The same with His command to walk in compassion and mercy: He has designed us with a corresponding yearning within ourselves to feel loved and accepted by others. And in commanding us to have no other gods before Him, He has already placed within us a desire to worship a God who dwells in mysteries beyond human comprehension— far above any gods constructed by our own means.

So, we can see that this high and mighty God is One who is thoughtful, benevolent and compassionate in His design. He instills in us a longing for good things, and at the same time, gives us the map that leads us to the place where our inward disposition is fulfilled. But that's not where this divine pattern ends! God's astute design of individual human beings is also His formula for a healthy, sustainable and just society.

When the Law (the Ten Commandments listed above, along with a host of supporting instructions for life) was given to Israel, there was no guarantee its recipients would take full advantage of its benefits by obeying it. In fact, the New Testament tells us just the opposite happens—the Law reveals how incapable we are of doing what is right, thus our need for a Savior, who came to us in Jesus Christ (see Galatians 3:24). Still, the way of life put in place by the Law continues to bring countless blessings to nations around the world because it was instituted on the principles by which God made the universe—righteousness, integrity, order and eternal purpose. As peoples and nation-states have implemented these principles, they have reaped the benefits that come from a lifestyle aligned with God's ways.

Unlike sinful ideologies and beliefs, God's commands demonstrate a valuing of human worth—of every individual in His sight. When the Law was given, it was only the lawbreakers who were appointed for destruction. Those who lived by the Law discovered the blessings of obedience, which carried inexhaustible benefits from one generation to another. As the Scripture says,

> But the mercy of the LORD is from everlasting to
> everlasting
> On those who fear Him,
> And His righteousness to children's children,
> To such as keep His covenant,
> And to those who remember His commandments to do
> them.
> Psalm 103:17–18

Additionally, God values men and women equally, people of all races equally and the young and old equally. Take a moment to consider how counterintuitive to selfish human nature the following God-given instruction is:

When you reap your harvest in your field, and forget a sheaf in the field, you shall not go back to get it; it shall be for the stranger, the fatherless, and the widow, that the LORD your God may bless you in all the work of your hands. When you beat your olive trees, you shall not go over the boughs again; it shall be for the stranger, the fatherless, and the widow. When you gather the grapes of your vineyard, you shall not glean it afterward; it shall be for the stranger, the fatherless, and the widow.

Deuteronomy 24:19–21

Similarly, the New Testament commands the taking care of orphans and widows as an expression of true religion (see James 1:27), and in upholding the value of all people, it says there is no distinction of value between Jew and Greek, slave and free, male and female (see Galatians 3:28). Though the Scripture affirms the concept of private ownership (of land and goods), it is always for the purpose of blessing one's fellow man in the process, and especially the unfortunate and forgotten, who are so easily subjected to further oppression in a dog-eat-dog world. In giving the Law, God's heart was to bless all mankind and the rest of His creation, and His heart has not changed to this day.

> We care deeply about law because we are so attuned to the issues of justice God addressed with the people of Israel.

The essence of the Law, in Jesus' words, is to "love the LORD your God with all your heart, with all your soul, and with all your mind," and to "love your neighbor as yourself" (Matthew 22:37, 39). Similarly, in summing up the Law and Prophets, He states what we know in our pop lexicon as "The Golden Rule": "Therefore, whatever you want men to do to you, do also to them, for this is the Law and the Prophets" (Matthew 7:12). Simplified to its most comprehensible foundation, this is what our worldview says about living among others in society. This, in its true expression, should inform everything that we do—on an interpersonal or global scale.

Judeo-Christianity Today

We have spent considerable time already on the phenomenon that is the United States of America because it identifies and even personifies Judeo-Christian values. It's possible to gain a decent level of understanding of the kind of world Christianity would spawn by taking a closer look at the history and ideals of the United States.

In case you haven't noticed, Americans are very law-based. We're obsessed with what is right and wrong, with how that should be decided, and with what to do when those standards are compromised. We care deeply about law because we are so attuned to the issues of justice God addressed with the people of Israel in the desert of Sinai so long ago. The qualities of impartiality, kindness and integrity seem universal to us—as if it would be impossible for anyone to think or feel differently. This, however, is far from the case. Simply look at the agenda being advanced by Radical Islam, in which the value of the individual (except for the ruling class) is pushed aside in favor of blind obedience to the sociopolitical dictates of a religious elite.

The entire basis of our law code is derived from Judeo-Christian principles—namely, the idea that individuals are responsible for their own actions and that they are free to chart their own destinies (as opposed to being born into a particular societal status from which they cannot rise). The concepts of the self-made man and the American Dream—in which people have the civil rights to make choices they feel will lead them to their desired end—are based on this understanding. We so easily take this for granted, assuming those in China, Indonesia, France and Turkey share this same attitude. But the truth is, in many

139

(even developed) parts of the world, individual freedom is more a theory than a reality.

Let us zoom in to take an up close look at a few of the most influential words in human history. In the American Declaration of Independence, the fathers of this nation wrote: "We hold these truths to be self-evident, that all men are created equal, that they are endowed by their Creator with certain unalienable Rights, that among these are Life, Liberty and the pursuit of Happiness."[4]

Has there ever been a more profound, liberating, empowering political statement written? And yet, within the statement of great freedom—freedom that spawned the Revolution that birthed the greatest nation in modern history—there is constraint that comes from being a nation *under God*. In this truth lies the key to individual and collective freedom.

"*We hold these truths to be self-evident . . .*" *Self*-evident—in other words, anyone can see these claims are valid, but it falls to someone to verbalize them so that we can all see, understand and agree upon a set of standards and conditions by which we should collectively abide.

"*That all men are created equal . . .*" All people—Black and Asian, Hispanic and Caucasian, Native American and European, men and women, model citizens and alleged murderers—all are created equal and should receive like treatment under the law.

"*That [all men] are endowed . . .*" Yes, but by Whom? "*By their Creator.*" The rights we speak of do not arise out of a vacuum. They are not granted by the cosmos or the stars or the environment or scientists or primordial ooze. They are granted by their Creator.

" *. . . with certain unalienable Rights . . .*" Notice, please, the qualification—"*certain* rights." Not *all* rights. Not whatever we want, whenever and however we want it. Certain rights. Thus, certain things necessarily exist to which we do *not* have the right.

" *. . . that among these are Life, Liberty and the pursuit of Happiness.*" These are the values we hold dear within the

Judeo-Christian frame of mind. *Where* each man and woman decides to look for and pursue this happiness is a personal choice, but the choice is each one's own nonetheless. The American dream might be more of a pipe dream or misguided platitude to some, but the *right* to dream is perhaps more important than the specific dreams to which we aspire.

From the early days, when Alexis de Tocqueville first noted the exceptional qualities of America, American Exceptionalism has remained a theme throughout our storied history. Not only is America the first modern democracy, the notion that there is something at the very core of America that sets it apart from other nations is, to many, as self-evident as the truths upon which our Founding Fathers built this nation. As opposed to other parts of the globe, which have been dominated by paradigms of social conformity and theocracy, America essentially owns the idea that freedom (personal liberties) should serve as the bedrock of society. It is this staunch belief in freedom that has led America (whether wisely or unwisely) to fight numerous wars on foreign soil—dying for the cause of others' liberty.

Of course we all know (and are reminded regularly by cynics) that America's attempt at this Judeo-Christian standard has been rife with double standards and countless mistakes. Certainly we have fallen short in living out our ideals—especially in our participation with the British slave trade. Nevertheless, those ideals have always been our objective, as well as the prophetic framework that allowed men like Dr. Martin Luther King Jr. the scaffolding necessary to right those wrongs and create a better society.

It is not my intent to deny atrocities that have been committed in the name of Christ, but rather, to denounce and expose them as heretical perversions of our faith. Moreover, the enormous focus that has been placed by Protestant and Evangelical Christians on identificational repentance (asking God and others for forgiveness for wrongs committed by prior generations) and movements in which Christian believers tread the paths of

141

Medieval Crusades to atone for the sins of their predecessors, attest to the fact that these past errors do not at all line up with the true essence of the Christian faith.

An important lesson we can glean from institutionalized Christianity is that the further a Christian expression distances itself from its Jewish roots, the more prone to corruption and distortion it becomes. America's founders (who sought to worship God freely rather than by human dictates) identified with the plight of the oppressed ancient Israelites, thus creating a distinctly Judeo-Christian heritage. Thankfully, America's unique legacy is largely free from the kind of anti-Semitism that plagued Medieval (and even modern) Europe. Many believe, as I do, that the primary source of America's unprecedented level of prosperity and influence is a direct result of our confessed dependence on God and our support of His people, Israel.

America's founders identified with the plight of the oppressed ancient Israelites.

Anti-Semitism Is Anti-Godism

From the outset of this chapter, we have discussed how the God we serve is the God of Abraham, Isaac and Jacob, the God who gave the Law through Moses and revealed Himself to a specific nation (Israel) for the purpose of blessing the whole world. The source of the freedom-loving society we live in today is a direct result of God's dealings with Israel. Quite literally, our Judeo-Christian worldview does not make sense unless it aligns itself with the Jewish people and the God of Israel.

So what does this mean for us today?

If we believe that God is faithful to His promises, then as a necessary consequence, we must believe that He is faithful to the promises He has made to Israel. After centuries of persecution

142

and dispersion throughout the world, in 1948, God made good on His promise to Abraham and the Hebrew prophets, to bring His people once again into the land that was to be forever theirs. Israel was reborn, and the world has never been the same. The testimony that God is alive, well and present in the lives of people and nations is an undeniable reality today due to His covenantal faithfulness to Israel. The flip side to this is the fact that those who are most opposed to God are also the ones most opposed to the Jewish people and the State of Israel. The reasoning behind this is that, if God's children can be done away with, then there would no longer be any proof of God's existence. As we know, all such efforts are, in the end, doomed to fail.

The more recent, ever-deepening level of relationship between the modern-day State of Israel and evangelical Christians is one that has been heavily scrutinized from all angles of the religious and political gamut. But the simple fact is, our worldview *by definition* supports and upholds a strong Israel, both because of the spiritual roots of our faith and also because of our commitment to live as a society that values freedom and democracy. The many evangelical groups that bring together pro-Israel believers to stand with the land and people of Israel show just how deep this conviction runs.

As we take this deep and penetrating look at the post-Christian world, we see how we have changed for the worse, shifting away from God's absolute, eternal promises. He, in the midst of mankind's meanderings, has stood unwavering. Nowhere do we see this demonstrated more clearly than in His dealings with Israel, and with those who have been grafted into the covenants of faith.

Three Keys to Judeo-Christianity

The truest indicator of Judeo-Christianity is, naturally, the two faith groups in and of themselves. It has never been more urgent that we, as Christians or God-fearing Jews, know *what* we believe and *why* we believe it—and above all, to know what we believe about God Himself. Let's review some of the central elements of this faith and ask ourselves how we're measuring up.

Prayer

In addition to the Bible, the foundation of the Judeo-Christian house is steeped in the value of prayer. For us, prayer is how we experientially know God and invite His presence into the workings of our lives and society as a whole. As part of our heritage from the Jewish people, prayer is what has sustained this people through unimaginable suffering, and it is how we know the God of Esther, Daniel and Elijah today. Prayer is intimately tied to the Scriptures, as Scripture itself contains many of the prayers that we use to engage the presence of God—in the Psalms and many other parts of the Bible.

> **Prayer is how we experientially know God.**

Passed down from generation to generation, the specific prayer known as the *Sh'ma* ("Hear"), found in Deuteronomy 6, has been the watchword of the Jewish people:

> Hear, O Israel: The LORD our God, the LORD is one! You shall love the LORD your God with all your heart, with all your soul, and with all your strength. And these words which I command you today shall be in your heart. You shall teach them diligently to your children, and shall talk of them when you sit in your house, when you walk by the way, when you lie down, and when you rise up. You shall bind them as a sign on your hand, and they shall be as frontlets between your eyes. You shall write them on the doorposts of your house and on your gates.
>
> Deuteronomy 6:4–9

In this prayer is found the declaration of who God is, and how this knowledge was to be passed on to future generations.

A few centuries ago in America, it was a foregone conclusion that God's ways (known through the Scripture and prayer) were best for individuals and nations, but this is no longer presupposed. Whereas our nation's school systems began in the 1600s and 1700s by educating our children directly from the moral code of the Bible, it is now all but illegal to pray in public schools except for once a year around a flagpole and perhaps a few marginalized extracurricular activities. We find the Ten Commandments being physically removed from the public sphere. When these things happen, does it cause us concern?

Not nearly as much as it should.

Worship in Song

An integral part of the worship experience in synagogue and in church has always been the use of song. So important is this aspect of worship that God made it a command to carry it out: "Oh, sing to the LORD a new song! Sing to the LORD, all the earth. Sing to the LORD, bless His name" (Psalm 96:1–2).

Why would God command His people to sing?

The impact of music and song on the human spirit is immeasurable—imparting a deep, nuanced quality that brings truths to life. In Jewish tradition, meditation on the Scriptures has typically been done in a style known as *cantillation,* which combines elements of chant and song. This has had a tremendous, enabling effect on the endurance of the Jewish people throughout centuries of persecution. In addition to glorifying God by involving our emotional being, song further commits His Word to our memory and releases His loving-kindness into our surroundings.

Christian history is rich with the heritage of those who have led worship of the Lord in singing. Handel's majestic "Hallelujah Chorus" from the great oratorio *Messiah* has been sung and applauded in countless settings, both Christian and secular. The great hymn writers of the faith Charles Wesley, Isaac Watts and

Fanny Crosby penned timeless words that, when put to song, have bolstered the faith of millions of believers. The spirituals sung by the African slaves instilled courage deep within them to continue to believe for their freedom in the midst of unthinkable adversity. If Scripture is the truth that anchors the Judeo-Christian house, and if prayer its vital activity, songs are the wings that allow our faith to soar and reach its fullest expression.

> We run the risk of our faith becoming something more about ourselves than it is about God.

One of my greatest laments is the loss of hymnody and musical integrity from the vocabulary of contemporary Christian worship. As I travel to dozens of churches every year, I detect a dangerous trend toward self-referential egotism. The three-chord choruses that pass for worship today are often more focused on ourselves than on the One we are supposed to be singing to. I love simple, intimate cries of devotion lifted to the Lord, but when we replace worship with navel-gazing, we run the risk of our faith becoming something more about ourselves than it is about God; something more subjective than eternal.

Family

As a vital building block of the Judeo-Christian worldview, the family was God's priority from the very beginning of creation. The first union between Adam and Eve served as a prototype for how God would interact with families for times to come: "Therefore a man shall leave his father and mother and be joined to his wife, and they shall become one flesh" (Genesis 2:24).

Continuing into His interactions with Israel, God's plan was always for families and tribes to be blessed, that they might be the building blocks for the nation as a whole. It has been said that a nation is only as strong as its families, and this has been true from the days of Moses until now. But the importance and validity of the traditional concept of family has come under severe attack. In one generation, our nation has attempted to redefine marriage, seeking to remove the authority of God's unequivocal mandate between a man and a woman. But the question is, can God's design for life and blessing still operate if you completely alter the formula?

In addition to the institution of marriage, the Bible gives us an unambiguous understanding of the value children bring to the family unit and to society at large. Alongside God's emphasis on the dignity of each life, the importance of children serves as the Judeo-Christian argument against the infanticide known as abortion, which has claimed the lives of over fifty million babies in America alone since the *Roe v. Wade* verdict in 1973.[5] Upholding the worth of these precious, defenseless babies, Psalm 127:3 says, "Children are a heritage from the LORD, the fruit of the womb is a reward." Throughout the Bible, we are instructed to nurture, disciple and train the next generation, and nowhere is this more evident scripturally than in the family itself.

Whether it be treatment of the poor, family structure or individual rights, the Bible gives very practical applications of truth. This biblical authority should serve as the single most important factor determining the social and moral code of the Judeo-Christian world.

We have spent the past three chapters studying three houses. Three worldviews. Three cultural kingdoms. Now, let us continue on to view each of these houses from another angle—one that will allow us to see them in a whole new light.

9

The Spirituality of the Three Houses

Thus far on our journey, we have committed considerable space studying the three houses. Now, we must turn our attention to observe the spiritual dimension within each one.

Spiritually Speaking

I always find it a bit odd when I meet people who describe themselves as "spiritual but not religious." I understand, of course, what they mean. They don't want to be identified with an institutional, traditional religion; they're not a "good Catholic," "on-fire Christian" or "practicing Jew." They want to be perceived as having an openness to the spiritual world that is not defined or limited by a specific creed, faction or value system. This commonly expressed sentiment in itself is not difficult for me to grasp. What I find odd is that which it unintentionally reveals about their attitude toward spirituality in general.

If someone chooses to identify himself as being "spiritual" he must likewise believe it is possible for a person to be "not spiritual"; that being spiritual is a choice—much like being Hindu or Muslim or agnostic. Such "spiritual" people would likely explain that they have a vague, indefinable connection to the spirit world. Equally, they would view an "unspiritual" person as someone who professes no interest or participation in any kind of spiritual reality.

> By denying or ignoring the spiritual realm, is it possible to truly disconnect oneself from it?

In this approach, spirituality is like a dinner party one can either opt in or opt out of attending. It is a prevalent school of thought that looks on the spiritual capacity as being voluntary. If you want to be spiritual, just RSVP; if not, just toss the invitation in the trash, forget about it and go on leading an existence void of any kind of metaphysical reality. Just as someone could walk away from Hinduism, saying, "That wasn't really for me," there are, perhaps, hundreds of millions of people who view spirituality as an elective sport.

Now that we have identified this underlying belief that spirituality is optional, we are able to question if that is, indeed, the case. Is it possible to walk away from all of spiritual reality in the same way someone would walk away from being a Buddhist monk? By denying or ignoring the spiritual realm, is it possible to truly disconnect oneself from it?

It is safe to conclude the answer is a definite "no." If you refuse to exercise in any way, you may become morbidly obese, but you will not become any less a "physical" being than you were before. Likewise, the desire to disengage from a spiritual reality—or invent one of your own—does not in any way remove you from the spiritual equation or allow you to escape its ultimate ramifications.

The Need to Believe

We humans seem to have ingrained into our genetic code an aptitude for the supernatural, which gives us a sense of meaning—a sense that our lives extend beyond what we can fully comprehend. Whether we call it a "life purpose" or "the greater good," we seem to be endowed with the need to believe in something larger, better and more enduring than ourselves. In fact, some medical researchers contend that our brains are actually "wired" for God. (See *Why God Won't Go Away* by Andrew Newberg, Eugene D'Aquili and Vince Rause; and *How God Changes Your Brain* by Andrew Newberg and Mark Robert Waldman.)

A friend of mine told me of a conversation she had with a relative around a holiday dinner table. This woman's sister-in-law is an educated, accomplished professional who has won numerous awards for her gifted design work. My friend, a Christian, was talking to her sister-in-law about the afterlife. Her sister-in-law responded by saying she did not believe in heaven or hell. She believed that after she died, she would become a star. When asked why she believed this, she shrugged, and said she didn't know why—she just did. Perhaps it was something she read in a novel or heard a character say in a movie once. Whatever the case, it was a comforting thought to her, and that was all she needed to solidify her opinion of eternity.

Although I have never personally come across any other people who believe they will become stars when they die, I'm sure there are more out there. I also imagine there are countless other theories that exist—each as individual as the ones who came up with them. With the surety of death awaiting us all, we are left to spend at least a portion of our lives wondering what, if anything, comes after the grave. The world's religions have offered a lot of theories, but they have not seemed always to satiate people's need for a sense of everlasting security. Especially when people are warned of a state of perpetual punishment that possibly awaits them, they often choose to abandon the whole heaven/hell scenario altogether in favor of something much less intimidating.

Reincarnation is a popular option. I suppose the idea of getting a "do-over" once you die is an attractive one to people who feel a sense of regret, hopelessness or insignificance in their (current) lives. Reincarnation also offers a feeling of connectedness—that we are all linked to one another by the interchange of consciousness that occurs from being reborn as another human being (or animal? or vegetable? or mineral?).

And if all else fails, what about good old-fashioned superstition? These pseudo-spiritual practices can be traced back throughout the centuries and seem primitive when we stop to think about them. But there are, I am sure, plenty of business executives on Wall Street, earning six-figure salaries and answering to no one but themselves, who will cross to the other side of the street before they dare walk underneath a workman's extension ladder.

Subjective spiritual conjectures aside, what can we make of those who claim they don't believe in an afterlife or in any spiritual dimension whatsoever?

It's a *Spiritual* World After All

The many who dismiss organized religion (and disorganized spirituality) often direct their spiritual yearnings toward other pursuits that don't claim to be sacred in nature. The amount of time, energy, finances, emotion and dedication that go into these other expressions prove that getting away from spiritual longings is not as easy as some would like to believe.

Take sports, for instance. Perhaps the Roman religious roots of athleticism hold more influence in modern big-sports culture than we realize. Intellectuals throughout the ages have acknowledged that sports traditions are not merely physical in nature but appeal to the spiritual dimension within us. All one need do is attend a Major League baseball game (or, for that matter, a Little League game!) to witness the phenomenon firsthand.

When thinking of a sports enthusiast, words like *passion*, *loyalty*, *devotion* and *zeal* readily come to mind. It's not uncommon for people to follow their favorite teams—to the exclusion of all others—for their entire lives. Conversion from one ball club to another can be deemed tantamount to betrayal—often resulting in an intervention by concerned family members and friends. Children are schooled not only in the art of sports, but in the code of belief that accompanies them.

But all this pales in comparison to the amount of force generated from the collective whole by placing their faith in a common goal. Packed stadiums pulsate with vigor as hundreds of thousands of fanatics scream and shout, or chant in unison. If someone, having absolutely no context for understanding it, witnessed this event, he or she would undoubtedly think that whatever was going on between those in uniform was a matter of life and death.

Although there is definitely a dimension of godliness that can be achieved through sports (virtues such as self-discipline, dedication and unity) it is clear how sports can be held in such high regard that they demand our worship. But if sports don't do it for you, there are plenty of other quasi-religious avenues to stroll down in one's quest for inner fulfillment.

Did you know, for example, that the majority of Americans believe pets have psychic powers? Pet owners believe their companions have the ability to foresee misfortune, perceive human emotion and predict natural disasters.[1] While there is scientific evidence to support some of these phenomena (such as guide dogs having the proven ability to sense chemical changes that bring about seizures in their owners), the idea of people paying a person on the street who is holding a cat they claim has extra-sensory powers to speak into their lives is a bizarre trend that is indicative of deeper societal issues.

There are, however, more accepted views of which the general public seems to be more fully convinced. These include the idea that we do, in spite of all appearances, live in a world where nice guys finish first, where the damsel in distress gets rescued in spite of wicked powers conspiring against her, and where dreams really do come true.

I'm referring of course to the happy endings of the romantic comedies we can't seem to get enough of. These Cinderella stories are what we are raised on, and while they are redemptive (an inherently biblical quality), divorced from the reality of God's saving power, they are mere fluff; fanciful wish fulfillment made to cash in on people's innermost hopes and desires.

This leads us to perhaps the most prevalent of all opaquely spiritual expressions: the self-help industry. From inspiration to motivation and from psychology to the New Age, sales of self-help titles skyrocketed in the 1990s and don't show signs of going away any time soon. This industry has found a way to tap in to our fuzzy, ill-defined spiritual yearnings and our obsession with self. We live in a therapeutic culture—one in which we are constantly searching for ways to understand and express ourselves. Realizing it's impossible for people to reach this level of catharsis without utilizing a spiritual component, the self-help industry has helped itself to the spiritual smorgasbord of pick-and-choose religion so prevalent in the West.

Titles such as these illustrate how easy it is to infuse man-made tactics with supernatural jargon:

- *Reinventing the Body, Resurrecting the Soul: How to Create a New You* by Deepak Chopra
- *The Power of Flow: Practical Ways to Transform Your Life with Meaningful Coincidence* by Charlene Belitz and Meg Lundstrom

- *Animals as Guides for the Soul: Stories of Life-Changing Encounters* by Susan Chernak McElroy
- *Awakening to the Sacred: Creating a Spiritual Life from Scratch* by Lama Surya Das

But the influence of this kind of do-it-yourself spirituality is not limited to one section of the bookstore; it is much more mainstream than that. Oprah has introduced this philosophy in friendly, unassuming packaging. Most Oprah fans do not even notice the spiritual undertones that lie beneath her middle-of-the-road persona. Consider the articles I came across by a quick trip to the "Spirit" page of Oprah's website:

- "Consciousness Cleanse Day 3: The Gift of Release"[2]
- "Living the Law of Attraction"[3]
- "How Meditation Can Save Your Relationship"[4]

With such a patchwork of spiritual practices, it is no wonder the biblical fabric from which many of them are cut is virtually unrecognizable. The further people progress down this path of personal enlightenment, the more distant they become from the idea that a singular, divine being with knowable attributes and a definitive, redemptive plan even exists.

> People believe in all sorts of random things—psychic pets, Oprah, the magic of a Disney theme park.

As we have seen, people believe in all sorts of random things—psychic pets, Oprah, the magic of a Disney theme park. Even when we try *not* to believe, we find it impossible. The bond between the spirit realm and us is so enduring that it pervades whatever area of our lives we care about most. In light of this, we can clearly see the certainty of a spiritual dimension influencing our everyday lives.

In a moment, we are going to take a close look at what fuels the spirituality of the three houses. But there is one more foundational concept we need to establish first.

The spiritual world and the natural world are undeniably linked. But the question is, what links them? What is the point of connection? What transfers spiritual "energy," if you will, into physical action? What life force is so elementary, so fundamental, so primal that it could serve as the bridge between these two dimensions?

The answer is very simple: blood.

Lifeblood

Blood is the most basic element of human life. Without it, we could not live. It's strange that blood is associated with dark, morbid things. Why is there a feeling of eeriness that comes along with talking about it? Blood is synonymous with life! As Scripture tells us, "The life . . . is in the blood" (Leviticus 17:11). On the other hand, I suppose it makes sense that we feel uncomfortable with the topic—that we often faint at the very sight of blood. After all, if blood is functioning properly as a life-giving force, it is invisible—hidden within our bodies. It is only when it has been spilled that we can tell something has gone wrong.

This bloodshed, of course, is often intentional. Knowing there is life in the blood, mankind has invented many ways to use blood as a way to manipulate the spirit realm. Sounds primeval, does it not? Downright barbaric. These rituals—often dark and chilling in nature—seem far removed from our advanced, sophisticated, modern lives; but are they? We are about to see how the influence of these three, modern-day houses is derived—consciously or not—through the principle of blood sacrifice.

Demanding Blood

In the West, we are far less familiar with the concept of blood sacrifice than people are in other cultures around the world. Part of our challenge as we deal with these topics is that they are often foreign to us. Our spiritual observances and practices of faith are much better managed and guarded—and our religious experiences are more polished than they are raw.

Such is not the case in the world of devout Islam and for those religious minorities who live in Muslim-controlled lands. Islam is built on the premise that everything you are and everything you own is to be used for the spread of Islam and the name of Allah. For children who grow up in an atmosphere in which they are taught nursery rhymes urging them to one day kill themselves and others in the name of religion, this is a tangible reality.

In the Shia tradition of Islam, the day of Ashura each year is a time to mourn the death of Muhammad's grandson Imam Hussein, who died in A.D. 680. During this observance, crowds of men take to the streets, where they hit their bare backs with chains and knives and strike their heads with swords. This gory display of self-flagellation causes them to bleed profusely and is a grotesque reminder of the death of Hussein. Though not observed by all Muslims, this holiday is a stark reminder of the violent self-subjugation required of those who devote themselves to Islam.[5]

As mentioned previously, self-flagellation also plays a part in the pilgrimage many devoted Muslims take to Mecca, where they pledge their allegiance to Allah and the global Muslim community in the ceremony encircling the Kaba.

But it's not only these types of Islamic traditions where a focus on blood is present. Children are spoon-fed the idea that violence is permissible if done for the name and purposes of Allah. The watchdog group Palestinian Media Watch (www.palwatch.org) has documented hundreds of videos shown on Palestinian TV that incite children and youth to violence through glorifying bloodshed. Many of these TV shows use puppets, interviews, games and songs to declare jihad against Jews, Christians, Israel and the rest of Western civilization.

In a radicalized context, Muslim children are taught that to sacrifice one's life (their own blood) by taking the life (blood) of others is the ultimate sign of devotion to Allah. A martyr or *shahid* who kills himself in order to murder "infidels" receives special praise and the immortal status of heroism, as well as (for males) the promise of a perverse afterlife full of sexual promiscuity.

Before going further, it would be fitting for us to examine how the Islamic faith defines the word *martyr*, as its definition differs significantly from what a martyr is in the Judeo-Christian tradition. In Greek, the word *martus* means to be a witness, and connotes dying to one's self—selfishness and pride—in order to humbly exalt Christ. Paul's exclamation, "For to me, to live is Christ, and to die is gain" (Philippians 1:21), speaks to this type of witness. On the other hand, to die as a suicide bomber and call that martyrdom as manifest in Radical Islam completely defiles the term *martyr*.

A chilling example of this other "martyrdom" mind-set comes from a woman by the name of Mariam Farhat, who, in affiliation with the terrorist group Hamas, was elected to the Palestinian Legislative Council in 2006. A professed mother of three suicide bombers, Mariam rejoiced in the fact that her sons gave up their blood for Allah and Islam. When asked about the others of her ten sons, she replied, "Allah be praised, I am preparing myself. I will sacrifice them all. If my duty requires me to sacrifice them all, I will not refuse—even if it costs me a hundred sons."[6]

It is not only the poor and disenfranchised who involve themselves in such blood sacrifices. It is also the wealthy, as we have seen from terrorism that takes place in developed nations—like the suicide bombers on July 7, 2005, in the public transportation system of London, England. These terrorists were highly

> Children are spoon-fed the idea that violence is permissible if done for the name and purposes of Allah.

successful members of British society who made the decision to give up their lives to murder others.[7]

What is it about Islam that motivates people to strap bombs to their backs and blow themselves up? I believe it's a spiritual reality, that wherever blood sacrifice is implemented in a culture, supernatural activity is present. Incitement occurs through many different avenues—television and Internet appeals, terrorist recruiting and religious speeches at mosques to name a few. Though these traditions would seem to us bizarre and even barbaric, they are widely practiced within Islam today in diverse nations around the world. To those who have been influenced by a culture of suicide and death, this darkness and evil is declared to be a praiseworthy and heroic display of devotion.

Blood of the Innocents

I'm sure this will come as no surprise, but the house of Militant Secularism also participates in this spiritual transaction, but in a way that has nothing to do with religion. In fact, their interactions with blood take place in a scientific dimension. Despite the sterile, harmless veneer over the surface of the abortion industry, it is nonetheless a shedding of blood that is integral to an ideological system affecting the hearts, minds and souls of millions.

Although there is much to be said regarding abortion on a moral and ethical level, that is not the focus here. Abortion is, in many ways, a black-and-white issue that has deeply divided this nation, and I am not in any way attempting to detract from the morality of this debate. I believe, however, that there is some room for agreement between concerned, ethically minded people regarding abortion regardless of where they stand on the issue. The sheer magnitude of the multibillion-dollar abortion industry and questionable practices of organizations like Planned Parenthood should be enough to raise questions in the minds of principled people.

No matter where they come out on the issue of abortion, even for those who once glibly quoted "a woman's right to choose" as their sole reason for support, it is becoming increasingly apparent that the issue is not so easily dismissed. The idea that a woman should have the right to choose whether or not to end another human life developing inside of her is a theoretical posture that does not account for the many ethical dilemmas that accompany any human undertaking.

What about motivation?

What about accountability?

What about money?

Within the last decade, much evidence has been brought to the public's attention that exposes fraudulent, deceitful, illegal and even racist policies and procedures long employed by abortion providers. I won't go into detail on this, as there is already an ample amount of writing easily accessible on the topic, but in addition to these disturbing findings, extensive health risks that affect the well-being of the mother have been discovered. Curiously, these health risks are not highlighted in the friendly image that abortion chains promote; but should we really expect a corporation to emphasize facts that are going to compromise its bottom line?

Politics and persuasion aside, many women's and men's feelings on the subject are changing on a purely personal level. No matter whether or not people believe in God, the right to life or abstinence outside of marriage, they seem to be much less likely to indiscriminately believe that abortion is a magic wand that makes "problems" go away. Since *Roe v. Wade* was decided in 1973, a second generation of Americans has come to childbearing age. This is the generation who grew up with the knowledge that their brothers and sisters had been aborted in the womb. Having witnessed or lived with the effects of abortion, this generation is much more wary of having abortions themselves and of those who promote abortion on demand.

Before we move on, I think it warrants mentioning the increasing level of brutality with which abortions are being carried out. The gruesome tactics used in partial-birth abortions, for instance, are enough to make even the staunchest proponent of abortion pause for consideration.

When I read about the case of a Philadelphia abortionist arrested on eight counts of murder and numerous other charges, I was not surprised. Shocked, yes, at the callousness and irresponsibility he exhibited, but not surprised in the least. Dr. Kermit Gosnell was charged in the death of a 41-year-old woman and seven infants who were allegedly born at nearly full-term after failed, illegal abortions. The babies are said to have been killed with a pair of scissors used to sever their spinal cords. The woman is believed to have died through an overdose of anesthesia in Gosnell's unsanitary, poorly run facility. The millionaire professional, who earned as much as $15,000 a day, is believed to have been operating in this fashion for years, illegally murdering hundreds of newborns.[8]

So much for our civilized, sanitized, bloodless culture!

So much for our civilized, sanitized, bloodless culture! I don't think it is hard to see how a society that does not value life could produce a doctor who kills infants in their first moments of it. Lest we digress from our main point, which is that the shedding of blood lends spiritual power that in turn supports corresponding ideological frameworks, allow me to spell this out unambiguously.

To get what we want, something has to be forfeited. If you want to bulk up in muscle, you're going to have to give up your couch time and junk food. In the same way, to live the life of your dreams—one in which you are not beholden to unforeseen commitments and held back by the needs of another—something has to be sacrificed. The blood shed through abortion is the sacrifice made in order to move forward the human will.

The house of secularism, which enthrones the human will above all else, considers its aspirations to be inerrant and its desires to reign supreme. Therefore, it seems only logical to them that a living being should be terminated as a matter of personal convenience. Such adherents often speak of abortion as a necessary evil. This always reminds me of the words Mother Teresa, an outspoken opponent of abortion, had to say on the subject: "It is a poverty to decide that a child must die so that you may live as you wish."[9]

Nothing But the Blood

The central message of the Christian faith is that we have been given eternal hope through the blood of Jesus Christ, who died in our place so that we can experience life. We believe the sacrifice of His blood covers our sins and brings healing, freedom and deliverance. Peter writes, "knowing that you were not redeemed with corruptible things, like silver or gold, from your aimless conduct received by tradition from your fathers, but with the precious blood of Christ, as of a lamb without blemish and without spot" (1 Peter 1:18–19). Because Jesus paid the ultimate penalty, satisfying the wrath of a just God, we don't have to earn God's approval by sacrificing our own lives or others'.

The blood of Christ as experienced symbolically in the act of Communion is a visible symbol and reminder of the power of redemption. When we share in the blood of Jesus by receiving His atonement, we invite His power to transform us from a place of hopelessness to a place of acceptance before God. "But now in Christ Jesus you who once were far off have been brought near by the blood of Christ" (Ephesians 2:13).

This blood of Jesus is a living, real sacrifice on the altar of heaven—it is a blood that, as the writer of Hebrews says, is better than that of bulls or goats in animal sacrifice (see Hebrews 9:12–14). Whereas the sacrifices described in the books of Exodus and Leviticus were temporary, the sacrifice of Jesus Christ is eternal. Jesus willingly sacrificed Himself once and for all (by allowing us sinful people to nail Him to a cross), and because He rose again from the dead, His is a living sacrifice that brings life to us.

> **This blood of Jesus is a living, real sacrifice on the altar of heaven.**

Jesus, then, is the Martyr whose blood still speaks today, and still brings healing wherever it is applied. Because He conquered death itself, He has the power to bring freedom and deliverance to all who call on His Name. Scripture describes Him as a sacrificial Lamb who, as He reigns on His throne in heaven, still bears the appearance of one who was slain (see Revelation 5:6).

Throughout the centuries, thousands of believers in this Lamb have followed Him in His death—not to atone for sin, but because of being persecuted due to their love and identification with Him. These are the true martyrs—those whose blood has been mingled with that of the Lamb, because they did not love their own lives even to death (see Revelation 12:11). Rather, they gave up their lives so that the message of life could go forth, even to their persecutors. Like Jesus, many of the saints who have gone before have prayed for their persecutors even while being killed by them.

Christian believers living under tyrannical regimes throughout history have faced persecution to the death at the hand of tyrannical rulers and governments of every age (*Foxe's Book of Martyrs* and *Extreme Devotion: The Voice of the Martyrs* are two examples of many sources documenting this history). The well-known declaration, "The blood of the martyrs is the seed of the church," is attributed to Church father Tertullian and well describes the impact of these lost lives.[10] It is true that their sacrifices have inspired thousands of believers who endure suffering, and that the effect of their lives has been planted like a seed, causing devotion for Jesus Christ to be multiplied.

For the many around the world today who call themselves Christians, this perfect blood, shed for the forgiveness of sins, is what gives motivation and power to everything they do. It inspires humanitarian aid extended by Christians to all peoples, regardless of contrary belief systems. This blood is why Christians pray and believe in miracles. It is what they celebrate, sing about and preach to everyone they meet—a message of life, not death. It causes them to live their lives as a "living sacrifice" unto God that blesses those around them (Romans 12:1).

As we have seen, each of the three houses has spiritual components because we are all, at the end of the day, spiritual beings. Having established this, let us take a comparative look at these cultures to determine which can hold up under scrutiny. After all, humanity is searching for a sturdy house in which to live. A place to rest, work, worship, raise kids. And they are looking for an eternal dwelling place. Which house can (really) deliver on all that?

> Each of the three houses has spiritual components because we are all, at the end of the day, spiritual beings.

10

Will the Real World Please Stand Up?

We are approaching the end of our journey together. I'm sure your mind is swirling with thoughts and images from the three houses we have studied. I hope that the incompatibility of these divergent worldviews has become apparent to you, and if it has, you are most likely asking yourself, *What's next?*

The Bible offers us key insights answering this question, but our quandary remains. Just how will the interplay between the absolutists and non-absolutists play out? Will the secularists be swept up into relationship with the God of the Bible through a massive spiritual revival? Will they yield to the stringent demands of Allah by adopting Sharia law? Will the secular, humanistic force create a one-world religion uniting the majority of Muslims, Christians, Jews and everyone else under a banner of false pretenses?

Whatever is about to happen, it seems that it is about to happen very soon—even that it is happening now. We've come to the end of the classic television game show *To Tell the Truth*, in which three contenders have done their best to convince the audience that each is the "real" person in question. Only one of the contestants can be right. The timer has buzzed, and I need to ask the inevitable question, "Will the real world please stand up?"

Putting aside political correctness, I will now candidly walk us through one final comparison of the three houses so that we can plainly see that the Judeo-Christian worldview is the best possible means of providing a platform of liberty for the human race. In contrast, we will see that the other two are not wisely built structures founded on immoveable rock, but foolishly constructed edifices built on sand, and doomed to collapse.

Contestant #1: Radical Islam

The notion that Islamic aggression toward the West stems from political discord or fiscal inequities imposed on the Arab world is a ruse. Regardless of other factors, the enmity disseminated by the Arab world is a result of how their religion teaches them to view us as "infidels" to be converted, conquered or killed in their quest to dominate the world system. Radical Islam will never be able to coexist peacefully with the non-Muslim world or with Muslims of different beliefs. The plain fact of the matter is that we cannot coexist with them because they refuse to coexist with us—or anyone who does not adhere to their archaic, totalitarian dogma.

> We cannot coexist with them because they refuse to coexist with us.

Consider the genocide and oppression of Christian minorities who have no political influence or power within Muslim majority countries. The subjugation and brutality these Christians suffer has nothing to do with politics! There is no political reason to massacre or persecute these innocent Christians. These acts should put to rest once and for all the assertion that terrorism is politically motivated, rather than what it is: an ideological and theological tenet of Islam.

Additionally, the terrorist attacks that have come to Western nations demonstrate that such acts do not originate from the attackers being societally disadvantaged. As mentioned before, the bombers in the deadly London attacks of July 2005 were well-educated, established professionals with successful careers, whose indiscriminate acts of violence originated from their radical Muslim beliefs and not from any underprivileged status.[1]

The Ultimate Goal

Islam's mandate to forcefully overtake secular and Judeo-Christian states and replace them with an Islamic regime is part of its genetic DNA. Even moderate Muslims who want to live according to Western values are ostracized, imprisoned or assaulted for opposing this violent, repressive system intent on taking over the world.

The 2011 assassination of Salman Taseer, the Muslim governor of the Punjab province in Pakistan, proves this point twofold. Mr. Taseer was killed by one of his own guards for supporting the release of a Christian Pakistani woman who was sentenced to death under the Muslim blasphemy law. Let's think about this: Someone in the Muslim world gets unjustly murdered for standing up against the unjust sentencing of a minority victim. Something about the way this culture operates just doesn't add up! Outside the courthouse where the trial took place, cheering crowds threw rose petals onto the vehicle transporting the killer.[2] As we can see in societies dominated by Sharia, even moderate Muslims are not safe.

One of my colleagues recently told of the following exchange by a seminary friend of his. The young seminarian had befriended a secular Muslim from Pakistan. The two got together regularly, and one of the times they were meeting for lunch happened to be during Ramadan—the month set aside for Muslim fasting.

Once the seminarian realized this, he apologized and suggested they reschedule their lunch date. But his Muslim friend insisted it was not a problem, explaining that if he were living in Pakistan, he would be fasting because Pakistan is a Muslim country. Since he was living in America, though, he felt no obligation to fast because America as a country was "not yet Muslim."

Now, there is more than one thing about this exchange that I find troubling. First, that this man's fasting does not seem to be done from the heart, but rather as a rote obligation done more as a means of achieving solidarity with other Muslims for political ends. This approach leads one to question whether fasting during Ramadan is viewed by Muslims as a means of personal consecration or as a tool to control those within Islam.

The second, obvious red flag for me is his final statement about America not being Muslim . . . yet. Yet? Is the idea that America will one day be an Islamic Republic a given to even secular Muslims? Does our fate seem inevitable to them? Unavoidable? Inescapable?

Many Westerners have conceded to this Islamist agenda as much as possible in hopes that they will learn to be content with a degree of political power. Appeasement, however, only adds fuel to the fire. Remember from chapter 6 the important concept in Islam that divides the world into the *Dar al-Islam* (house of Islam) and the *Dar al-Harb* (house of war). In the mind-set of Radical Islam, there are only two types of nations in the world—those who are already Islamic, and those who will be. To show a sign of weakness in the presence of this Islam (through land secession or the altering of Western laws) is only to enable radical Muslims to fully achieve their goal of a worldwide Muslim caliphate.

Human Rights and Wrongs

To us in the West, the phrase "human rights" is something deeply ingrained in us from an early age. As those born into nations ensuring democratic freedoms, the idea that all people deserve to be treated with decency and respect is a lesson we're supposed to learn on the playground as we all wait as equals to take our turns.

> The idea that all people deserve to be treated with decency and respect is a lesson we are supposed to learn on the playground.

You yourself may have traveled, at your own expense, to a foreign nation on a service project in which you worked to improve the quality of life for those living in poverty. The principle of self-sacrifice—of reaching out to extend hope and help—should come naturally to us raised in the Judeo-Christian tradition. It stems from the belief that God has created every person, and they therefore have inherent worth. The images that remain fixed in our minds and the stories we hear from others who return from these missions stay with us for years, and they motivate our giving, our prayers and our continued service. It's worth pointing out that even secular humanists who deny the existence of God, but who nevertheless find themselves living on the foundation of a godly culture, often adhere to this practice of altruism—albeit selectively.

Sadly, though, human rights are entirely unheard of in many parts of the globe. Whether one-party dictatorships, multi-party regimes or traditional Islamic rulership, the Arab world is rife with conflict—especially with women and minorities struggling for basic civil liberties we Westerners take for granted. Often, where human rights are espoused, they are regarded as offensive, absurd—even blasphemous.

If you have any doubt about how appalling living under Sharia governance would be, you need only to look at the long list of atrocities and human rights violations openly sanctioned in the Muslim world. Two of the foremost examples are Saudi Arabia, a Sunni Muslim kingdom that funnels millions of dollars into covert Muslim infiltration schemes in the West, and the Shia nation of Iran, which has continued ominously on its nuclear proliferation campaign, threatening the existence of Israel and America. Both Saudi Arabia and Iran (and many other Islamic nations) have a dark history of human rights abuses, such as sanctioned acts of violence against women and against the so-called infidels who are not a part of Islam.

- Not long ago, a Red Cross worker in Afghanistan was sentenced to execution by hanging for converting to Christianity. Tragically, this is typical in countries in which Muslim law has authority.[3]
- In the United Arab Emirates, the highest court of the country issued a ruling in 2010 that upheld Muslim men's right to beat their wives. An article published by CNSNEWS.com reported on the discussion that has since ensued on just how much force is permissible for men to use while beating their wives, plus other aspects of "beating etiquette."[4]
- Women in the strictly-Islamic nation of Saudi Arabia must fully veil themselves (including their faces) when out in public. This, however, is not enough for the Saudi religious police who in 2010 issued an order stating that women with "seditious eyes" must cover them up.[5]

And lest we think these examples are only in nations far removed from the West, consider this ridiculous ruling from Austria in December 2010:

- A court ruling fined a man 800 Euros for yodeling while mowing his lawn because it offended a neighboring Muslim who charged that it sounded similar to the Muslim call to prayer. The accused man stated it wasn't his intent to

169

insult anyone; that he was yodeling simply because he was in such a good mood.[6] If this kind of ludicrous kowtowing is tolerated in über-liberal Europe, what does this say for the future of nations making room for Muslim legislation?

In the Islamic world and Muslim-majority nations, human rights are, to some, laughable, and to others, a far-off dream. Even in recent years, parties in nations such as Sudan, Algeria and Afghanistan have thought nothing of killing immense numbers of their own people to gain advantage. To them, there is no standard of measure equally applied to all, so a "might makes right" attitude prevails. For those born into wealth and privilege, it's a "winner-take-all" situation in which the rich and powerful are not held accountable for their actions, but are instead encouraged to live extravagantly. For the disadvantaged, there is little compassion extended for their needs, and they grow ever more exploited and disenfranchised.

Contrasted with the corrupt, totalitarian regimes and power structures of Islamic nations, Western benevolence is unthinkable—a thing to be taken advantage of as a sign of weakness. This may sound basic to you—so evident it doesn't warrant mentioning. But however elementary these concepts may seem, it's important to keep in mind that the majority of Westerners live in a bubble of self-defeating naïveté and refuse to believe that those who profess to hate them actually do.

While there are definitely double standards and many other points of concern that exist in Western nations, these misdeeds are, at the very least, sharply criticized, if not punished under the rule of law. Whether or not it is followed, the standard we Westerners are held to is that the more wealth or privilege you enjoy, the more responsibility you have to use it for good.

On the heels of the unthinkable comes the unthinking house of Militant Secularism, which first denigrates life-giving values and then paves the way for Radical Islam to come in and finish the job. Ironically, these misguided relativists are too blinded by their own moral equivocation to see that they will be the first victims of Islam's brutally intolerant policies the moment these radicals get the chance.

I will never forget an image I saw recently. The photo showed radical Islamists protesting outside the Israeli embassy in New York; no surprise there. But I noticed that, for some inexplicable reason, there were homosexuals under a rainbow banner of "gay pride" thrown into the mix. The fact that these two groups were united together by their unfounded hatred of Israel is one issue. The question it raises is this: Do these homosexual U.S. citizens, who enjoy the same law-protected life as everyone else in America, realize what would happen to them if they went to an Islamic nation and engaged in a homosexual lifestyle?

> America oddly enjoins these two opposing crowds by creating a society in which they are protected (from each other) under law.

But the Judeo-Christian values operating within the state of New York provide the freedom for these two otherwise-irreconcilable groups to protest side by side. The unique Petri dish that is America oddly enjoins these two opposing crowds by creating a society in which they are protected (from each other) under law. How can militant secularists (which those in the gay community generally are) not see that by accommodating the agenda of the radical Islamists they are endangering themselves?

Contestant #2: Militant Secularism

Secularism is a scourge on society in that it deprives cultures of their spiritual beliefs while replacing them with its own. In the chapter on Militant Secularism, we saw how humanism is actually a religion, but one that poses as a secular force so that it has a broader sphere of influence. Once it has gained the upper hand by painting "religious" people as dangerous extremists, it is free to dominate prevailing culture with mores that match its unprincipled way of life.

Instead of distinguishing between healthy religious culture and unhealthy religious culture, the secularists' strategy is to throw the baby of religion out with the proverbial bathwater in an attempt to relegate religious sensibility to the graveyard of humanity.

There are probably several reasons for this. One reason is that mandating an irreligious society is a much easier task than doing the moral work required to hold on to a sacred value system. If you think about it, it's actually very convenient for people to corporately write God out of the script of existence if they have already decided to do away with Him on a personal level.

A second reason is that it is hard to define problematic religious actions as absolutely wrong if you don't believe in absolutes to begin with! It is much easier to conclude that religion itself is the problem, and that a purely secular culture is the answer. People who draw these conclusions are the ones who then go on to draw naïve parallels equating "radical Islamists" with "radical Christians."

Religiously Irreligious

As we have seen, the tenets of secular humanism fulfill all the criteria of a religious system: behavioral standards, rituals, an authoritarian hierarchy. The fact that its values are vacuous, its philosophies shoddy and its morality bankrupt does not negate the fact that it does, for better or worse, possess values, philosophies and morality (of a sort).

The ironic thing about the followers of such secular doctrines is that they believe themselves to be the most irreligious people on the face of the earth. They consider religious conviction beneath them—unsophisticated, irrational, even primitive—not

172

realizing they are more religious than most religious people could ever claim to be. Have you ever "gotten into it" with a moral relativist? Rarely have I seen people argue their beliefs with such vehement gusto, such fervent passion, such abject rage. To describe their antics as anything less than "religious zeal" would not do them justice.

Those who claim there is no objective, definable standard by which to measure "right" and "wrong" always intrigue me. They will argue their position endlessly. I suppose their disregard for absolutes goes into effect the moment after they have established the one absolute needed for their world to work: *there are no absolutes.* Their mantra? *"The only truth is that there is no truth."* Once they have convinced their opponent of this, they are content to let them win every successive debate. This ritual has always seemed suspicious to me—a little like a child who dismisses whatever is said about them by telling their opponent, *"Whatever you say bounces off of me and sticks to you like glue."*

Personifying this is Christopher Hitchens, a prominent face of the "New Atheism." This controversial radical rejects the "atheist" label, preferring instead to be called an "anti-theist." He views the concept of God as not just stupid but actually detrimental to the human race, hence the title of his book, *God Is Not Great: How Religion Poisons Everything.*

Secularists gain yet more clout by uniting divergent streams of thought into one raging river. They succeed at this because they don't embrace any one particular premise or guiding force. Rather, these evolutionary humanists are interested in where they are headed, in what they are capable of. For this reason, anyone willing to surrender their absolutes gets drafted into their game. They don't mind putting up with some New Age fluff here or there—as long as their new teammates agree not to let their spirituality go beyond the realm of personal opinion.

Humanism's objective is to deny there is any other ruling force in the cosmos other than the human will. They are more than willing to bend the rules to increase their manpower. Humanists, after all, have their work cut out for them. The weight of the universe resting on the shoulders of humanity is no small burden. There's a lot for them to accomplish, and to a staunch humanist, the end more than justifies the means.

> Humanism's objective is to deny there is any other ruling force in the cosmos other than the human will.

By disqualifying faith-based sentiment from the public sphere, secularists have disseminated their morals (or lack thereof) to billions who have taken the bait hook, line and sinker. If their friend Karl Marx was right, and religion truly is the opiate of the masses, then our contemporary secular world is in a constant hallucinogenic state brought on by the ceaseless and unrestrained promulgation of the humanist faith.

Religion du Jour

Well, it finally happened. All the Christians, moralists and other thinkers who have spent the last fifteen years trying to convince everyone that Oprah is not just a friendly talk-show host but actually a spiritual guru manipulating the minds of the unsuspecting and doling out moral counsel on a mass scale can breathe a sigh of relief. They have, unfortunately, been proven right. Using her billionaire status, the media mogul has joined forces with fellow New Age seeker and bestselling author Eckhart Tolle in spawning an establishment named the New Earth Church.

Although Oprah's credo is not humanist in the strictest sense of the term (due to embracing pantheism and supernatural components), the compatibility of the two is apparent. Both religions (humanism and New Age) place *self* at the center of existence and embrace the idea that goodness comes solely from within us—whether from human nature or from the god within us all. New Age beliefs are so loose that diverse and even contradictory views are accepted within its circle: reincarnation, Transcendental Meditation, extraterrestrial life, astrology, spirit guides and earth/goddess worship are just a sampling of the many paths to an enlightened consciousness, which is the essence of a New Ager's concept of salvation. Its belief structure is so fluid that convictions can be adopted or abandoned at will.

In chapter 9, we contemplated the appeal this brand of spirituality has in today's world. For now, suffice it to say that the anything-goes attitude of the New Age tribe lends itself very well to the intents and purposes of the self-directed humanist agenda.

> Environmentalism has become so closely tied to globalization, the two are essentially synonymous.

Speaking of agenda, the secularists have found the perfect cause under which to finally unite humanity in its counterfeit utopia. They have identified the faltering state of our ravaged environment as the logical excuse for us to hang on to each other for dear life. Environmentalism has become so closely tied to globalization, the two are essentially synonymous.

Gone Global

Think back to chapter 2, which looked at "The End of the World As We Know It." There we made an in-depth assessment of several key environmental hazards. Because the many ecological crises earth is facing are happening simultaneously, their effects are compounded, and the resulting natural disasters are wreaking havoc on the already-fragile biosphere. Politicians, corporations and ideologues understand this, and they see that people's fear of environmental catastrophe motivates how they vote, buy and think. Thus they use environmental causes to influence public opinion.

Identifying people's incentives and catering to them is by no means a novel concept in business or in politics. Banding together to save the planet, however, has become a universal leveraging device, which those who don't believe in anything but themselves are using strategically to advance their worldview. In fact, they have gone so far as to fabricate scientific data to make these issues seem worse than they actually are.[7]

If the condition of our planet really is as bad as it seems, why would people feel the need to falsify information making things appear worse? It's because they have an agenda they are pushing, and it has more on the docket than environmental causes. I hope you can see the red neon light over this situation flashing "Danger! Danger! Danger!"

Al Gore makes the connection between environmentalism and globalization explicitly clear in a guest appearance he made on the sitcom *30 Rock*—a politically charged, humanist propaganda tool. The episode he appeared in was in honor of "Green Week," in which the characters were working to reduce their carbon footprint on the environment.

Posing as a janitor installing eco-friendly fluorescent lightbulbs, the former vice president and presidential candidate offered the following advice:

> If we're going to solve the climate crisis . . . we've got to change the laws and policies through collective political action on a large scale. You know, there's an old African proverb . . . [that states,] "If you want to go quickly, go alone; if you want to go far, go together." We need to go far . . . quickly.[8]

To Al Gore and his counterparts, globalization is the only answer; a last-ditch effort at saving the earth by ourselves and for ourselves. Although I am all for wisely preserving natural resources and cherishing the beautiful planet that has been created for us to steward, I cannot pretend that my motivation in doing so is remotely similar to that of radical, agnostic militants who want to save the planet because they have "nowhere else to go."

Despite the green revolution becoming a fashionable (and indeed marketable) phenomenon, the idea that we can reverse the incalculable damage done to our planet simply by starting to recycle our plastic water bottles is naïve and mistaken. These issues run deep, and correcting them will require much more than humanity is, at this point, able or willing to give. This is not to say that many gifted and well-meaning people will not try, but will their efforts achieve their intended effect, or will they only serve to contribute to the corrupt agenda of a globalized political machine?

Contestant #3: The House of Judeo-Christianity

This brings us to our final contender. The house of Judeo-Christianity is an unlikely candidate for global ascendancy, considering its founder never envisioned dominating others through force. But paradoxically, this humble faith has come to influence the lives of virtually everyone on the planet. It has become a source of inspiration and revolution—a reason for its believers to fight for freedom. Evangelical Christianity has enjoyed a meteoric rise to global preeminence due to the authentic, transformative power of this simple way of life.

The questions become apparent: Will Christians and Jews re-embrace the true essence of their faith by substantiating it with biblical action and fueling it with the presence of God? Or, will they relinquish all influence over the free world (which was built on the foundation of their value system) to forces that will lead humanity into a new Dark Age? It seems the answer to these questions dangles by a thin thread of hope; for in many parts of the world the once-great house of Judeo-Christianity lies in ruins.

A Change in Trends

Consider these insights from George Barna, one of the most distinguished students of America's religious trends and founder of the Barna Group. He conducted several polls that reveal the current state of the American evangelical church and how it lacks a clear understanding of a biblical worldview.

- Only 4 percent of all American adults have a biblical worldview as the basis of their decision-making.
- Only 9 percent of born-again U.S. Christians have such a perspective on life.
- Only half of America's Protestant pastors—51 percent— have a biblical worldview.[9]

Furthermore, the percentage of Americans who identify themselves as Christians has significantly declined since 1990, as the 2008 American Religious Identification Survey report reveals. The percentage of self-identified Christians went from 86 percent to 76 percent over the last two decades, with most of this decline coming between the years 1990 and 2001.[10] Even though many of these Christians may have been Christian in name only, this figure still points to an alarming deterioration of our social fabric.

Additionally, the Barna Group has published findings indicating that among young adults (ages 18–23), less than 1 percent ascribe to a biblical worldview that affirms beliefs such as the existence of absolute truth, the complete accuracy of the Bible and that God is the omnipotent, omniscient Creator who governs the universe.[11]

Likewise Western Europe, once the cradle of Christian civilization, is now essentially wholly secular, as it continues to move into what has come to be called a post-Christian culture. When you visit these countries of the European Union, where a belief in God was once commonplace, it's difficult to find any trace of Him at all. The churches are largely empty and more like museums than vibrant houses of worship. In fact, some of these remarkable historic buildings are being converted into mosques or day spas! The population of historically Christian people groups continues to plummet as these Westerners cast off traditional values (namely marriage and child-rearing) in favor of short-term cohabitation and what could justly be termed fast-food abortions. The statistics on

> The churches are largely empty and more like museums than vibrant houses of worship.

birthrates are sobering. These countries seem to be fulfilling a self-imposed death wish brought on by birthrates well below replacement levels.[12]

As this decline climaxed around the turn of the 21st century, another trend emerged in different parts of the globe. Continents not characteristically Christian saw an enormous surge in Christian population, often in the face of overt persecution. In an article citing statistics provided by David Barrett and the Overseas Ministries Studies Center, Christianity.com documents the explosion of the Christian faith in African nations:[13]

	% Christians in 1900	% Christians in 2000
Congo-Zaire	1.4%	95.4%
Angola	0.6%	94.1%
Swaziland	1.0%	86.9%
Zambia	0.3%	82.4%
Kenya	0.2%	79.3%
Malawi	1.8%	76.8%

Asia, too, is a continent embracing Christianity in spite of Communist opposition, with a sudden increase in the number of those who identify themselves as followers of Jesus. This largely Protestant, Pentecostal phenomenon is concentrated in house churches and estimated to number more than one hundred million, with as many as ten thousand new converts every day![14]

We can clearly see the composition of Christianity changing drastically, and if it proves to be as influential a force in shaping Eastern societies as it has Western ones, Christianity may end up as a primary influence in world events for decades to come. But where does this leave Westerners? The Western world, once largely Christian in its composition, has become the platform from which monotheistic (and specifically Christian) values are silenced or marginalized. Is this the legacy we want our children and grandchildren to inherit from us?

Is America a Christian nation? Oddly enough, while many Americans might say no, radical Muslims from other parts of the world would certainly say yes, and they point to America's shortcomings as a consequence of the spiritual stance this nation has taken. But in the end it's not what anyone else says, but what Americans themselves say, which will most influence what way of life we adopt as our own. If our culture becomes something other than what we desire it to be, we have no one to blame but ourselves. If the culture around us has changed, then by definition it is we who have changed, because our priorities and values have driven (or at the very least, allowed) the changes we see around us.

Rediscovering Righteous Roots

Perhaps you've heard the story of how one of America's most prestigious landmarks received its well-known inscription. Located in a grassy, central square of the Harvard University campus in Cambridge, Massachusetts, the historic Emerson Hall is home to the school's philosophy department. It is said that the faculty of that day were eager to choose an inscription for their new building that would befit the intellectual pursuits that were to go on inside it. So, the professors, philosophers and

180

other intellectuals got together and agreed upon a phrase that seemed an accurate theme to the scholarly endeavors of philosophy, psychology and the like. They drew from early Greek thought, settling on the Protagorean maxim, "Man is the measure of all things."

When the faculty returned from their summer recess, however, they discovered that the president of the university had overridden their recommendation and inscribed an entirely different motto. The story goes that President Charles William Eliot was so incensed at the presumptuous attitude of his peers—the idea that human beings were the center of the universe—that he chose a quotation that expressed a completely contrary outlook. And if you were to visit Harvard Square today and approach the great steps of Emerson Hall, you could look up and still read that inscription, engraved in the stone above. It reads: "WHAT IS MAN THAT THOU ART MINDFUL OF HIM?"[15] The wording of this age-old question is taken from the eighth Psalm. Directed toward the Creator of the universe, it reminds all of us of our insignificance, our weakness and our humility before God.

The American founding fathers concur:

John Hancock:
    In circumstances as dark as these, it becomes us, as Men and Christians, to reflect that whilst every prudent measure should be taken to ward off the impending judgments, . . . at the same time all confidence must be withheld from the means we use; and reposed only on that God rules in the armies of Heaven, and without His whole blessing, the best human counsels are but foolishness.

    —From "A Day of Fasting, Humiliation and Prayer,
    with a total abstinence from labor and recreation,"
    a proclamation on April 15, 1775[16]

Benjamin Franklin:
    God governs in the affairs of man. And if a sparrow cannot fall to the ground without His notice, is it probable that an

empire can rise without His aid? We have been assured, Sir, in the sacred writings, that "except the Lord build the house, they labor in vain that build it." I firmly believe this; and I also believe that without His concurring aid we shall succeed in this political building no better, than the builders of Babel.

—From a request for prayers
at the Constitutional Convention of 1787[17]

If there has always been a struggle initiated by people against their Creator to deny their need for Him (or to deny Him altogether), that struggle seems to have reached a deafening crescendo in this hour. The war being waged by militant secularists, who claim we are the measure of all things, and by radical Islamists, who assert their repressive religious regime as the measure of all things, has reached its zenith.

The United States of America is essentially the last safe harbor of freedom on earth. If America as we know it ceases to exist (which is looking ever more certain to be the case) our children will either end up wearing burkas and bowing their knee to a false god or heading for the hills to escape a system of worldwide control seeking to monitor all that is bought and sold, which the secularists are eager to enact.

Do we understand what is at stake? Are we willing to pay the price required? Are we willing to stay awake and remain active to ensure that the torch of liberty is not extinguished on our watch?

I always find it chilling to hear one well-known and well-circulated axiom regarding the great civilizations of the world. It seems to describe our predicament exactly:

[The world's great civilizations] have progressed through the following sequence:
from bondage to spiritual faith, from spiritual faith to great courage,
from courage to liberty, from liberty to abundance,
from abundance to selfishness, from selfishness to complacency,

182

from complacency to apathy, from apathy to dependency, from dependency back to bondage.[18]

As Islamization escalates in Europe, and brings all that comes with it (terrorism, human rights abuses, racism, sexism and tyranny), it becomes more obvious that multiculturalism is no longer an option for those who wish to continue to live in freedom. One example of the kind of thing I'm referring to is an instance when a Spanish teacher was sued by a Muslim student for speaking on the cultural topic of Spanish ham.[19] There is no shortage of ridiculous examples like this, although many have a much more somber tone because the victim is not sued, but instead killed, maimed or raped.

The heads of state in Germany, France and the United Kingdom have each done an about-face on the subject of multiculturalism. Just recently, these distinguished leaders have, one by one, publicly stated that their nations have erred in promoting segmented multiculturalism within their borders, particularly in light of the dangerous advancement of Radical Islam in Europe. All three leaders pointed to the need to uphold their national identity and values among all who immigrate, so as to guard against the rise of these destructive patterns in their communities.[20]

The sad irony is that tolerance, multiculturalism and diversity in their modern forms originated as uniquely American ideals. True coexistence is possible, in measure, if all parties involved agree to abide under a moral law that binds them together. This is the core philosophy behind the making of America. This is why I refer to tolerance and multiculturalism (in their authentic forms) as American virtues. This is what makes efforts to expunge Christian values from public life incomprehensible. We all but invented these ideas! They are the building blocks of American civilization. To have a nation founded on freedom—pledged to protecting the rights of its citizens to express differing beliefs and cultures even when the majority does not hold these views—is a novel and very progressive concept. It was, specifically, the belief in a just God who lovingly created the world and everyone in it that prompted the American experiment to begin with.

But instead of learning from the disastrous mistakes of the European humanists who sacrificed their liberty on the altar of pluralism, many Americans seem intent on following in their footsteps. Case in point: Feisal Abdul Rauf, the Muslim imam responsible for promoting the Ground Zero mosque, was one of the nominees for *Time* magazine's "Person of the Year" in 2010.[21] And similarly, NBC named Sharif El-Gamal, the Ground Zero mosque developer, as "Person of the Year" the same year.[22]

> To have a nation founded on freedom is a novel and very progressive concept.

As we have seen before, the answer militant secularists offer is more of the same: humanism worldwide through globalization. Thirty-two U.S. Senators and 92 U.S. Representatives proved this point when they signed the Declaration of Interdependence on January 30, 1976: "Two centuries ago our forefathers brought forth a new nation; now we must join with others to bring forth a new world order."[23] Sounds like a nice theory, but disconnected from their Source, the values of our forefathers no longer hold godly authority, and so, make way for another means of power to take hold.

Some more sobering facts to consider: "The Muslim population in Britain has grown by more than 500,000 to 2.4 million in just four years, according to official research collated for *The Times*." The Office for National Statistics reveals that this means the Islamic population in the U.K. has grown ten times faster than the rest of society. What's more, "In the same period the number of Christians in the country fell by more than 2 million." And, "while the biggest Christian population is among the over-70s bracket, for Muslims, it is the under-4s."[24]

Listen to what a British citizen has to say about the situation in the U.K.:

Christianity is under siege in this country. Britain's national religion has never been so marginalized and derided, especially by the public institutions that should be defending it. . . . [A] new form of virulent secularism is sweeping through society—and its target is Christianity. . . . It is no coincidence that as Christianity is repeatedly attacked, so the social fabric of Britain becomes increasingly frayed. As we lose our strong moral compass, family breakdown and violent crime are at record levels while our once famous sense of community spirit is evaporating.[25]

Poignant. Yet a revered church leader or devout Christian activist did not speak these words. They were spoken by Dr. Taj Hargey, chairman of the Muslim Educational Centre of Oxford and imam of the Summertown Islamic Congregation. In an article entitled, "What Has Britain Come To When It Takes a Muslim Like Me to Defend Christianity?" Dr. Hargey issued this word of warning to a sleeping Church and a Christian society so anesthetized by political correctness that it cannot stand up for itself amidst the most blatant offenses.

Unquestionably, anyone willing to acknowledge these global trends has the moral obligation to speak up—to stand up—against this insanity while we still have the chance.

11

God's House

ou may be scratching your head at this chapter title: *God's House? Is God's not the house of the Judeo-Christian worldview?*

The kind of dwelling I'm referring to here as *God's house* is not the same kind of structure as the house of Radical Islam, the house of Militant Secularism or even the house of the Judeo-Christian worldview. God's house is not a cultural Kingdom, so much as a countercultural force.

We have spent much energy focusing on the houses people have built and continue to construct. But in the midst of all this—in the midst of the rise and fall of nations, the interface of world cultures—there is something taking place behind the scenes. Silently, steadily, sovereignly, God is building a house. In the midst of what *they're* doing, what *we're* doing and what anyone thinks *anyone else* is doing, *God is building a house. His* house. And His house is the one that will stand.

You see, we have spent the duration of this book studying the three primary cultural houses operating in the world today.

We have weighed their philosophies against their practices, their roots against their fruits, to see which worldview would best sustain a free world in the years to come. And the discovery that the absolutist house of Judeo-Christianity is the only viable choice comes as no surprise to most of us, I'm sure. But I want to make an important clarification to this conclusion, lest after having come so far, we lose our way at the end. God is not the great Santa-Claus-in-the-sky who is there to give us back our Judeo-Christian house for Christmas; in fact, it is quite the opposite. God is not here to build *our* house; *we* are here to build *His*.

> **God is not here to build *our* house; *we* are here to build *His*.**

Fit for a King

Imagine you are a real estate agent whose job is to find the perfect residence in which God will abide. Talk about pressure! Where would you even start? A stunning, six-story beachfront mansion suddenly seems inadequate for the One who holds the oceans in the palm of His hand (see Isaiah 40:12). A majestic, ornate Tuscan villa barely suffices for a toolshed for the One who laid the foundations of the earth (see Job 38:4). You get the idea. He's seen it all, done it all. In fact, He *made* it all. All of the splendor, influence, intellect and might humanity can muster is not a drop in the bucket to God. God Himself asks:

> Heaven *is* My throne,
> And earth *is* My footstool.
> Where *is* the house that you will build Me?
> And where *is* the place of My rest?
> Isaiah 66:1 (emphasis added)

That has the potential to sound like a God no one could relate to. Even One who is petty or picky or difficult to please. But this is far from the case. God does not issue this declaration as a way of cutting us off from Him, but rather as a way of showing us who He is and what it is He truly desires. In the next breath, God answers His own question about where He desires to dwell.

> But on this *one* will I look:
> On *him who is* [humble] and of a contrite spirit,
> And who trembles at My word.
>
> Isaiah 66:2 (emphasis added)

Right here, we have the exact description of the kind of house God is in the market for. And as the book of Acts confirms, "The Most High does not dwell in houses made by human hands" (Acts 7:48, NASB). The simple fact is that we cannot give anything to God. Except ourselves. It makes sense that the Lord Almighty—the King of Glory—would not want anything from us except that which we choose to give Him through pure motives. He doesn't *need* our money; He doesn't *need* our talent; He doesn't even *need* us! But He loves us and wants to be in relationship with us. He wants to receive what comes from our hearts, because what He truly wants to give us is *His* heart.

Clashing Kingdoms

The ancient kingdoms of Saul and David make the contrast between an empty structure and a vibrant house abundantly clear. Saul and David both reigned as kings of Israel in the years of the undivided kingdom, and the prophet Samuel anointed both to this position. The hearts of these two rulers were set on very different things, however. A look at the circumstance under which they first met (the story of David and Goliath) reveals a theme that would be carried throughout their entire lives.

The regal King Saul, who had been appointed to his position specifically for the purpose of delivering the Israelites from the Philistines, is found incapable and ineffective at accomplishing

God's will. He is unwilling even to face the enemy. His great, sophisticated army seems strong in the flesh, but against a giant (supernatural) threat, it is utterly powerless.

Enter David—a lowly shepherd boy—the youngest of all his brothers. He comes onto the scene with no real training. In fact, he came there only to serve, by bringing nourishment to his brothers, who were accomplished swordsmen and trained for battle. But this young shepherd boy had a very different reaction to this menace than did Saul and all his soldiers. David took one look at Goliath and said, "Who *is* this uncircumcised Philistine, that he should defy the armies of the living God?" (1 Samuel 17:26).

After having gained the blessing of Saul, whom we can imagine cowering amidst his armor, David, *unarmored*, famously takes down his towering opponent, saying, "You come to me with a sword, with a spear, and with a javelin. But I come to you in the name of the LORD of hosts" (1 Samuel 17:45). David, with a single stone, was able to do what all the armies of Saul could not, because David had true knowledge of God and true faith in God.

I find myself thinking a lot about the difference between Saul and David these days. While Saul represents what is possible with mankind, David represents what is possible with God. Saul was always doing things in his own strength, while David was always accomplishing far greater things through the strength of God. This caused Saul to grow very jealous of David, and to hate him unjustly. The reason David had the capabilities he did was because he had a relationship with God, while Saul did not. Insecure and self-seeking, Saul put his energy into preserving his own house—his own family line—not caring remotely for the house of the Lord. Saul was intent on his own well-being and set himself up as the center of the kingdom. By contrast, the first thing David did after becoming king was to win back God's holy city, Jerusalem. David wanted to be aligned with God's heart, and that meant seeing the Lord's vision for Zion restored. He was only able to do so, however, after a long, bitter saga between him and Saul. Let us reflect on this foundational narrative from the Old Testament in order to gain more clarity about what the difference between Saul and David means for our own lives.

As we have already discussed, Saul was not at all interested in doing things God's way. He was carnal and compromising. He did not have the fear of the Lord, but the fear of man. This people-pleasing spirit is what prompted him to offer up an unlawful sacrifice to God (see 1 Samuel 13:6–11). He showed no regard for the real spiritual authority God had set in place (Samuel, the priest), deciding instead that he could do it on his own. This defiance of God ultimately cost Saul his kingdom. He was rebuked by Samuel, "But now your kingdom shall not continue. The Lord has sought for Himself a man after His own heart, and the Lord has commanded him to be commander over His people, because you have not kept what the Lord commanded you" (1 Samuel 13:14).

> Saul was not at all interested in doing things God's way. He was carnal and compromising.

After this, while Saul was still king, God fulfilled what Samuel prophesied by having David anointed to be the next king of Israel. But this was not the end of the kingdom of Saul! This is because kingdoms—systems, structures, processes, ways of thinking about and doing things—can continue on long after the anointing has left them. This was the case with the kingdom of Saul. Saul maintained his position of influence, but the Spirit of God had left him and was raising up another leader who would, this time, do things God's way.

Laying It on the Line

The reason I draw our attention to this, here at the end of our journey, is because I believe that the same dynamic is happening in the Judeo-Christian house today. There is a people-pleasing spirit that has long since infiltrated this worldview. It dates back to the first centuries of the Church, in which paganism was mixed with the pure expression of faith in God through Jesus Christ. This synchronistic mixture has compromised the way of life Jesus brought to the earth and introduced a false root system, which has produced toxic fruit and much evil in every age since. Many Church reformers, revivalists and earnest servants of God have sought to bring correction to the Body of the Lord in every generation. These efforts have been made to restore us to biblical spirituality, as opposed to continuing to labor under a cultural system that can too easily amount to religious futility.

Do you see how the house of David and the house of Saul, which we just studied, mirror this state of affairs? The house of Saul, with all its prestige and carnal resources, and the house of David, with its simple devotion to the heart of God. I am not in any way suggesting that the Body of the Lord should not have influence, clout and established ways. On the contrary, since God created mankind to rule and reign upon the earth (see Psalm 8:6), those of us who have been restored to right relationship with Him should be the best equipped to do so. We need to become those the world looks to for answers. God will give us favor, inventiveness, wisdom and strategy if we put our faith in Him alone. We should be people of influence, but we better be sure that our true status comes from God, and not from man.

We need to take inventory. We need to get our house in order! I see so clearly a dividing line coming to the house of Judeo-Christianity even as we speak. The sword of the Lord is coming to judge the false root system, which has spawned much of what falls under the umbrella of "Christianity." From Vatican City to the non-denominational country chapel, the Church of Jesus Christ universal is coming to a moment of divine separation between what is of God and what is not. The Church is being redefined, and the difference between those who are intent on their own interests and in compromising the Word and ways of God for the sake of popular opinion, and those who, at any cost, will lay down their own lives and self-wills to bring glory to Him, is becoming more and more apparent.

Have you noticed, for instance, the trend in the Church today to make God "relevant" to prevailing culture? As if the Creator of the universe somehow became irrelevant to His creation! I understand the need to re-present the Good News to the world in a way that makes sense to them, but if in the process of doing so we lose the eternal, abiding truth we are trying to communicate in the first place, we have obviously missed our mark.

Increasingly, I feel that opening up the Bible and reading from the prophets is like turning on the television to catch the evening news. With each passing day, it seems God's Word is more powerfully accurate and actively confrontational than ever before. I am utterly astonished at how a book written thousands of years ago could have such exacting import on the world centuries later. Ironically, I find that those who dedicate their lives to *making* the Bible seem relevant to the world are often some of the most detached and irrelevant people I have ever encountered. Their self-made kingdoms are elaborate artifices, but inside, they lack enduring substance. We must remember that the Word of the Lord is like food, like oxygen, like water. There is no life apart from it.

Fabricating palatable interpretations of God's Word and focusing on popular acceptance in the society at large only succeeds in producing shallow, immature believers who usually are not quite sure what they're supposed to be believing anyway.

But back to our biblical parallel. The essential difference between the houses of David and Saul was that David's was an absolutist worldview, and Saul's was relativistic. Saul's commitment to the Lord's house was only relative—He obeyed God to the degree to which it served him and was convenient for his own kingdom. Saul's house was one of mixture—a perfect example of God's people not living according to God's ways. David (though imperfect) sought to honor God absolutely. As we just saw, David restored the centrality of the Ark of God's presence, bringing it into the middle of Israel and instituting true worship as the nation's central priority.

Just as the children of Israel, during the kingdoms of Saul and David, were faced with a dilemma, we too are faced with a moment of decision. They had to choose between one kingdom and another, and so do we. Remember when King Saul was seeking to kill David? David was forced to run for his life, to hide in caves and cry out to God every step of the way. The people had to choose whether they were going to stick with Saul or embrace God's anointed, who didn't have much going for him at the time. They had to choose between what was familiar, comfortable and functional for them, and the word of the Lord. There was nothing (by human estimation) that would make David seem like the better choice. All David had was the anointing, the promise of God that he was called to lead His people into His Presence. David had fresh oil; Saul had everything else. Whom would you have aligned yourself with?

> **If we do not get the mixture out of our own personal lives and out of our corporate spiritual life, we will not be able to exist at all!**

Friends, it is very true that we cannot coexist with those who want to harm us, but it is just as true that a kingdom divided against itself cannot stand (see Matthew 12:25). Our own house is only as secure as its foundation. We will find that, if we do not get the mixture (sin, compromise, idolatry) out of our own personal lives and out of our corporate spiritual life, we will not be able to exist at all!

The reason that visionary people left the corrupt, tyrannical religious and political systems of Europe to establish a country where freedom could reign was so that they would be free to follow God's ways. Men and women did not risk their lives and die to establish this country so that it (and the evangelical Christianity inexorably intertwined with it) could become a place known for harboring morally lazy, money-hungry, self-serving degenerates! The United States of America was meant to be a land where the inhabitants would be free to worship, free to evangelize, free to serve and give and govern righteously. We have witnessed firsthand the disastrous results that come from losing sight of our original purpose.

For this reason, we must ask ourselves, "How much does our house today line up with God's house?" God promises that if we will make His house a priority, then (and only then) He will bless ours. Hebrews 3:6 speaks of God's house, "whose house we are if we hold fast the confidence and the rejoicing of the hope firm to the end." And how do we hold fast that confidence and joy until the end? By living as David and others have done, as a persevering, dedicated house of prayer, offering up the living sacrifices of our lives as continual worship and prayer.

Because we act as if biblical spirituality is a smorgasbord from which we can pick and choose as we please, the world gets the message that God is open for negotiation, interpretation and conciliation. We have to keep in mind: *The Kingdom of God is not a democracy.* God is not the president of the United States. You didn't vote Him in, and you're not going to vote Him out. We are mistaken if we believe that God must line up with our house. No, we must line up with His. The house of Judeo-Christianity, in actuality, should be a dwelling place in which we can find God's presence, both now and in eternity.

We are faced with the question of how the house of Judeo-Christianity will be defined on our watch. Like the Israelites who lived during Saul's and David's reigns, *we are a transitional generation.* We are being presented the opportunity to bring reform and restoration to the Church, so that the Church can build a house for God that He truly desires to dwell in. A spiritual revival that unites the Church and ignites us to fuel God's purposes is what has saved this nation in the past, and I promise you, it is the only thing that can save it again.

What About Us?

At the very outset, we contemplated these words of Jesus, who rebuked some of the leaders of His religious community because they missed the forest for the trees. He couldn't get over their spiritual blindness and inability to perceive God's heart for their generation:

> "When it is evening you say, 'It will be fair weather, for the sky is red'; and in the morning, 'It will be foul weather today, for the sky is red and threatening.' Hypocrites! You know how to discern the face of the sky, but you cannot discern the signs of the times."
>
> Matthew 16:2–3

And what about us? Are we any different?

We know how to get along in life—how to take care of ourselves. But do we understand the big picture of what is going on around us—of why we're here in the first place? The signs of the times are right under our noses. They are hard to miss, but people continually try. As we can see so clearly from this passage, and throughout the entirety of Scripture, God desires His people to be aware and active. He wants them to know what His Spirit is doing so that His purposes are not thwarted or hijacked by those who don't have humanity's best interests at heart.

My hope is that the information you have gained from reading this book will provide tools for you to navigate through the ideological minefields of current cultural kingdoms. My hope is that you will live by revelation and not by reason—that you will walk by faith and not by sight. As the saying goes, you are called to be a *thermostat,* not a *thermometer.* A thermometer merely *gauges* the temperature of a situation. A thermostat, on the other hand, *sets* the temperature of the air around it after detecting what changes are needed in the atmosphere. Ask yourself which you are—the thermostat or the thermometer.

If you have any doubt in your mind, let me verify for you: You are called to be a thermostat—an atmosphere-changer everywhere you go. This is why you have been born; this is why you are here—not merely to survive, but to thrive; to be transformed by the power of God and to extend that transformation power to everything and everyone around you. *So much depends on this.* There are people only you can reach. I can't reach them. Your pastor can't reach them. Joyce Meyer can't reach them. They are people—neighbors, cousins, bus drivers, schoolteachers, pregnant teens, homeless veterans, cashiers—whom God has placed in your path. People *I* will never meet. People who are waiting to receive the Gospel of salvation and take their place in the Kingdom of God.

You are the agent of change you have been wanting to see in the world today.

Do you see? *You* are the answer; *you* are the strategy; *you* are the agent of change you have been wanting to see in the world today. There are places only you can go—unique locks to which you are a perfectly matched key. Your mission in life is to hear and obey God's voice. It is to be strong and do exploits (see Daniel 11:32). It is to give yourself to Him by using your gifts and abilities to the max. It is to make every day count.

And do you know how you can start? In the place of worship and prayer. No one else can sing *for* you; no one else can worship *for* you. There is a victory that has been won over your life that you alone have the power to apprehend and set in motion. This world is waiting to receive the blessings that God has to impart through you. Everything the enemy of your soul has used to try to bring you down and shut you up are your tickets to overcoming in the battle of life through the blood of the Lamb and the word of your testimony (see Revelation 12:11). You may not be much in your own estimation, but in the hand of God, you are a like a secret weapon designed to tear down the work the enemy has done. Are you waiting to *feel* ready? Are you waiting to *appear* brilliant? Are you waiting to *be* perfect? If so, you may be waiting quite a while.

- Was Esther—the orphan queen—well equipped to take down the greatest threat her people had known in its recent history?
- Was Abraham Lincoln in prime position to become one of the greatest presidents in United States history, after suffering the death of his mother at age nine, and having to work tirelessly (and futilely) to save his family farm?
- Was Rosa Parks—the middle-aged seamstress—well positioned for success when she refused to give up her seat to a white passenger and move to the back of the bus?

Everyone—absolutely everyone—has a realm of authority, a sphere of influence. Whether you're 22 or 92, you have been called to the Kingdom for such a time as this (see Esther 4:14)! Become God's mouthpiece. Become His hands and feet. Pray the prayer that only you can pray, and watch God take your humble offering and use it to impact the masses. If you still question whether or not your one life, your one soup kitchen, your one prayer group can make a difference, I want to remind you of a vitally important aspect of our faith: Faith. That is not a typo; the vitally important aspect of our faith *is faith*.

Did you ever notice how, throughout Scripture, God gained victories for His people against long odds? He set up countless battles and challenges in which there was no way for His people to emerge victorious except that they placed their faith in Him. These long odds typically reflected the fact that those on the Lord's side were vastly outnumbered.

The Few

Whenever I speak to groups on the topics we have been discussing in this book, I inevitably find myself reaching for a Bible, holding it up high and announcing, "From cover to cover, this book is the story of *the remnant*."

The Word of God is filled with stories, page after page, chapter after chapter, generation after generation of the majority getting it wrong, and only a small minority getting it right. It gives account after account of one individual, one family, one little group heeding the voice of God and, through their intercessory obedience, paving the way for God's plan of righteousness and redemption to be brought forth to the nations.

- Joshua and Caleb maintained a faith testimony in keeping with the Word of the Lord and, though they had to wait their whole lives, eventually led the people of God to possess the Promised Land (see Joshua 14:1–15).
- Gideon underwent an enormous challenge. God intentionally thinned out the numbers of his vast, capable army to prove that victory comes not by might, nor by power, but by the Spirit of the Lord (see Judges 6–7).
- Another formidable war was won in the most unlikely of circumstances, when the leader of the opposing army was slain by Jael—a woman who was just going about her daily business inside her own tent (see Judges 4:17–23). Can you imagine the headlines announcing that a housewife had won the war?
- The 120 bedraggled and disheartened men and women who huddled together in the Upper Room took the Good News of salvation to all of Israel, under the miraculous power that crossed language barriers and caused thousands to come into the Kingdom in a single day (see Acts 2).
- Noah was ridiculed by his neighbors when he built a larger-than-life-sized boat in his backyard. Can you imagine him trying to explain to them the voice he heard, which told him to do so? Yet it was Noah's family that God spared and used to repopulate the planet (see Genesis 6–9).

In the midst of an unfaithful majority, God has purposed in His heart to preserve for Himself a remnant who will remain faithful and allow His Kingdom to advance in the earth.

If you're holding this book in your hands and resonating with its message, you are one of a precious few willing to be the rudder God can use to steer the ship of humanity away from the oncoming iceberg. My prayer is always for God to give me eyes to see and ears to hear what the Spirit is saying to the Church. This is my prayer for you as well. I know that the Spirit of wisdom and revelation is longing to unlock heavenly mysteries appointed for this hour. And I count it a privilege, as I hope you do, to live in a generation uniquely poised to receive them.

> God has purposed in His heart to preserve for Himself a remnant.

Before we conclude our time together, there is one last thought I want to offer you. One last puzzle piece that will complete the image we have been studying so diligently. In the midst of the clash of cultures and uproar of kingdoms, which are all shouting "Coexistence!" there is one word being carried down to earth by the breath of God in response to all this. It is a word of hope, a word of authority, a word that means *peace*. That word is *Shalom*.

12

Shalom

I t may seem that a chapter called "Shalom" is a strange way
to conclude a book about the myth of coexistence. But it is
fitting that God—the Maker of the Universe—would be the
One to have the final word over it. And that word is *shalom*.

As we have explored the present-day culture war of the three
houses, I want to leave you with a picture of the true ending of
the intense battle I have described. In these final pages, we will
be considering what the word *shalom* means, and what it means
for our lives. We will continue to discover what, exactly, God's
house is, and how we can ensure the house of Judeo-Christianity
genuinely reflects that.

By now we understand that we are part of a cultural mêlée. We
are engaged in ideological warfare. We are spiritual combatants
in the existential battle raging in the nations of the earth. But
what exactly is at stake? What are we fighting for? If coexistence
is a myth, what is the reality?

A House of *What?*

We have considered, at some length, precisely what the house of God is. And what does God Himself have to say about His house? A very specific answer is given in Isaiah 56: "For My house shall be called a house of prayer for all nations" (v. 7). God's house is a house of prayer. In its full expression, God's house is not self-referential, but rather is designed to be a source of life, blessing and change for all the nations of the earth.

Notice that God did not say, "My house will be called a house of *preaching* for all people." Or, "My house will be called a house of *programs* suited to all demographics."

People have attempted to make God's house conform to their standards rather than conforming their standards to God's. We have filled God's house (which is intended to be the resting place of His Presence) with all sorts of substitutes when God gives us such a clear mandate in His Word.

This Scripture from Isaiah is so central to the heart of God that it's the very one Jesus quotes when He cleansed the temple in His day (see Matthew 21:12–13). He was filled with righteous indignation at what His Father's house had become. The people who should have been receiving instruction and renewal were instead being exploited and led astray. True worship had been compromised. Jesus overturned the tables of the money changers in the temple courts to make a definitive statement against the hypocrisy and lawlessness that had tainted this holy people.

Today we too need to be zealous for truth and righteousness amidst the company of believers. We should be judging *ourselves,* not the world. There needs to be order in the house of God (see 1 Corinthians 14:40). Everyone is invited to be a part of this house—it crosses all racial, ethnic, gender and societal barriers. But anyone who desires to come into the house of God must be willing to part with every lesser thing. See, God is not obligated to cooperate with us simply because we hang a sign on our door. Just because we name a building after Him does not mean God is required to come inside. On the contrary, anything we have built apart from Him will be demolished. The apostle Paul says:

> According to the grace of God which was given to me, as a wise master builder I have laid the foundation, and another builds on it. But let each one take heed how he builds on it. For no other foundation can anyone lay than that which is laid, which is Jesus Christ. Now if anyone builds on this foundation with gold, silver, precious stones, wood, hay, straw, each one's work will become clear; for the Day will declare it, because it will be revealed by fire; and the fire will test each one's work, of what sort it is.
>
> 1 Corinthians 3:10–13

Remember: We are supposed to be building God's house—not our own. His house is a house of prayer, a place of consecrated intimacy. He is searching for those who will abide in the place of prayer, believing as Simeon did in the temple until the prophetic promises are fulfilled (see Luke 2:25–32). God's house should reflect Him—not our man-made philosophies and traditions.

God is not obligated to cooperate with us simply because we hang a sign on our door.

This house of prayer is also known as the house of David. David was determined to see God's Kingdom authority established on the earth. No cost was too high; no sacrifice too great. Listen to these words from one of David's psalms: "Zeal for Your house has consumed me." (Psalm 69:9, NASB). And because of this zeal, God made a covenant with David, which He promised would endure for all time: "Your house and your kingdom shall be established forever before you. Your throne shall be established forever" (2 Samuel 7:16).

David—the young shepherd boy who became Israel's greatest king—had an exceptionally close relationship with the Lord.

This relationship would come to define the nation of Israel not only in his own time, but for time immemorial. You see, David *got it*. He understood what God was after. God wants the earthly to mirror the heavenly. He wants the pattern of His temple here on earth to reflect the pattern of His dwelling place in heaven. And what is that? What is going on in heaven even now and for all eternity? *Worship*.

A Rebuilt Tent

David's house—the tabernacle of David—was a place of worship and prayer, a place of unfettered devotion in the Presence of God. This was David's priority. He couldn't wait to get the Ark of the Covenant back in the central place it was meant to be.

David's tabernacle was not an impressive building. In fact, it was merely a tent. But God was not concerned about that—He liked what was going on inside. David, along with the priests and Levites he appointed, led God's people in extravagant, wholehearted worship. They sang tirelessly, danced raucously, shouted, knelt, clapped and lifted up skilled music to God. They did this constantly—24 hours a day, 7 days a week, 365 days a year. This Davidic worship was the key to Israel's success and well-being.

> What is going on in heaven even now and for all eternity? Worship.

After that season came to an end, Israel enjoyed some periods in which Davidic worship was restored. These revivals were always accompanied by military victories and societal reformation. God was so touched by the unbridled love demonstrated through this worship that He made a special promise to restore it one day for good.

> On that day I will raise up
> The tabernacle of David, which has fallen down,

And repair its damages;
I will raise up its ruins,
And rebuild it as in the days of old.
Amos 9:11

Friends, this one verse of Scripture has apprehended me for the better half of my adult life. I have wept it, prayed it, taught it. My spirit has been stirred by these words because I perceive an anointing on them for our generation. I firmly believe that the time prophesied in this Scripture is upon us. I believe *"that day"* is *today*. When Jesus came as Messiah in fulfillment of thousands of years of prophetic longing, He was called the Son of David (see Matthew 15:22; Mark 10:47), testifying that God's ancient dealings with this extraordinary individual were covenantal promises that will never be broken.

Never forget—David's house was, literally, just a tent. What God promised to resurrect is the spirit of worship and prayer that pervaded that ancient house. At the end of the age, there will be a people who, like David, *get it*. They will be a people of worship. A people of prayer. A people of His Presence.

God promises that His house on earth will be built after the pattern of His heavenly home; that it will be a place of worship and prayer 24 hours a day, 7 days a week, 365 days a year. There, people understand that prayer is not optional, not peripheral, not something to relegate to a group of 62-year-old intercessors who meet in a back Sunday school room on Tuesday evenings. Prayer is our lifeline—our connection to God. It was never meant to be an activity, but a lifestyle. In fact, prayer is supposed to be our very identity.

Wherever God's Presence is not prioritized among His people, we see prayer dying out, and the spiritual vitality of the people dying along with it. Once abandoned, the structures that contained the house of God begin to decay themselves. After the spiritual life dissipates, people eventually stop going through the motions. First the pews become vacant. Then the buildings crumble or close.

To combat this phenomenon, some choose to respond in the flesh, which only results in disguising the problem, not fixing it. To maintain appearances, many do away with God altogether in favor of popular opinion; they offer a vanilla message that has no delivering power because it is void of the cross, the blood and the truth of Jesus Christ.

Many do away with God altogether in favor of popular opinion.

Beloved, a full parking lot is not God's measure of success! He is much more concerned with the character of Christ being formed in us. Ninety-minute Sunday-morning Christianity is not sufficient for the hour of trial that is upon us. Unless we truly offer people the one thing we have going for us (God's Presence), we will, sooner or later, lose them no matter how many camels we have in our drive-through Christmas nativity.

Although I see both the empty-church scenario and the misleadingly-full-church scenario at work in our day, I also see another reality arising. Throughout the nations, there is a pressing into prayer as we have never seen before. The nation of Brazil has experienced massive Christian revival in prayer and worship. The Chinese church never stops crying out and has multiplied at an unprecedented rate in the last century. Christian prayer gatherings of multiple millions can be found in African nations like Nigeria. Large venues in Europe are filled on days dedicated to global prayer. The tabernacle of David is being restored in our day.

Prayer Wars

There is a reason Jesus prayed these words to His Father: "Your kingdom come, Your will be done on earth *as it is in heaven*"

(Matthew 6:10, emphasis added). The answer to the earth's problems is heavenly. And it becomes manifest only when we intercede sacrificially and dedicate our lives to pulling the answers, resources, blessings and miracles out of heaven and onto the earth. The place of ceaseless adoration of the uncreated God from ages past to ages hence is the place that contains all we need for the challenges our complex, contemporary world is experiencing.

Prayer is the vehicle that moves eternal realities forward.

When we gain authority in the heavenly realm, we see transformation in our families, cities and nations. Intercession is the key to the ministry of reconciliation with which God has entrusted us. This is why every force known to man is intent on keeping God's people from truly relating to Him—from truly praying to Him and being in His Presence. Prayer is the vehicle that moves eternal realities forward and gives them power and authority in this realm.

But we would be mistaken to think that God is the only one building a house of prayer. Do you realize that the other two houses we have been studying are also houses of prayer? Yes, prayer works both ways. Prayer is really just heart-energy directed to any outside source—whether to Yahweh, Allah or Oprah.

In the chapter dedicated to the spirituality of the three houses, we clearly saw how human beings are spiritual entities—that we are hardwired with a need to believe. It should not surprise us, then, to discover that the house of Radical Islam, the house of Militant Secularism and the house of Judeo-Christianity are all spiritual powerhouses that, in one way or other, offer humanity a way to channel their spiritual vigor toward something beyond themselves.

It is not difficult to see that the house of Radical Islam is a house of prayer. Wherever they are, whatever they are doing, five times a day, they drop to their knees and pay homage to their god. The United States was attacked on September 11, 2001, by a house of prayer. Radical Islamists who perform the unthinkable acts of warfare against civilians do so out of religious devotion to Allah. Around the world on 9/11, radically religious Muslims rejoiced in the streets, and imams gave victory speeches because of their corporate violent triumph. The house of Radical Islam, at its center, is a house of prayer.

It may, at first, seem curious to refer to the house of Militant Secularism as a house of prayer, but a closer look reveals this to be the case. As we so clearly saw, humanism functions as a religion. Its mission is to dominate all that have not bowed their knee to its dogma by eradicating the Presence of God from all sectors of society. Like the other two houses, the house of Militant Secularism is fueled by the beliefs and actions of those who follow it. It thrives on their heart-energy. It gains power when people live by its creeds. Although humanists would not pray to God, they are praying to something. Themselves. Their careers. The earth. Evidence of this is everywhere you look. MTV is pumping out—24/7/365—*music and a message*. The house of Militant Secularism is a house of prayer.

And what about us? Are we a house of prayer? We are called to be, but as we have seen, the majority of what passes for Judeo-Christianity is everything *but* true prayer and worship in the Presence of God. The house of Adonai—the house of the Lord—is at a pivotal juncture. There is no time for indecision, no place for compromise, no room for neutrality. We will either be hot or cold. We need to fulfill our calling!

Coming to Him as to a living stone, rejected indeed by men, but chosen by God and precious, you also, as living stones, are being built up a spiritual house, a holy priesthood, to offer up spiritual sacrifices acceptable to God through Jesus Christ.

1 Peter 2:4–5

We are biblically instructed to be a holy priesthood—not a holy evangelism team, not a holy theology club, not a holy acoustic guitar concert. Our primary calling is to minister to Him in His Presence. I'm not talking about attending a service. *I am talking about giving our lives to the purposes of God.* We are called to come alongside one another in unity, to bring our gifts and strengthen the work of the Lord.

I have dedicated the majority of this book to examining the multifaceted issues that are defining our world today. I have done my best to illustrate the three primary players on the world's stage with the intent of providing us with a framework for understanding the days we are living in.

Now, in these last several pages, I am saying something that might seem counterintuitive. All this talk about prayer might seem to contradict the overall content of this book. We have been talking about current events, but as we close, I want to shed the light of eternity on those events to ensure we are seeing them in proper perspective. So many threads are woven into this global fabric—religious, political, economic, educational—but what is the heart of the matter? What is it that everyone is really after? Is it money? Land? Oil? Fame? What is the true cause of the existential battle we find ourselves in—the reason for the wars raging in the earth? I would submit to you that everything we see going on around us cannot be properly understood until we see it for what it is: a battle for worship.

Worship *is* something. Worship *does* something. Worship is what is going on in heaven, and what, if there is to be any hope for us, must happen in the earth. But not only is this fact tied to our hearts, it is tied to the earth itself. The question is not only, "Whose Name will be lifted up over my life?" But, "Whose Name will be lifted up over the Temple Mount?" Yes, that one ancient piece of earth means something in a way that nothing else does.

Throughout this book, we have exposed the existential framework behind the everyday. We have uncovered the spiritual realities that intersect with our media, values and daily routines. We can clearly see that there is more to current events than that which is merely current. So, it should come as no surprise to find that there is a geographic center to the spiritual universe.

The Holy City

Our journey has led us to Jerusalem—the crossroads of the world. This unique city is unlike any other place on the planet. It's difficult to describe how distinct and singular its atmosphere is. Although most urban centers are a confluence of varying ethnicities and cultural expressions, the thing that sets Jerusalem apart is the sense that its very location is the reason for the convergence of the diverse people who populate it. Its composition is not arbitrary or incidental. Its inhabitants did not happen upon this landmass due to natural migration patterns or random chance. Rather, it seems that each and every person who resides in this land does so by deliberate, intentional choice. No one is there by accident. If you live in Israel, it's because you believe something so strongly you are willing to stake your life on it. Many end up doing just that.

There is a geographic center to the spiritual universe.

Often thought of as the crossroads of the three monotheistic faiths, the charged religious nature of Jerusalem also positions it at the hub of world politics. Jerusalem is not an easy place to live. There are no comfort zones in Jerusalem—nowhere to hide. The irreconcilable philosophies hurled down through the ages at avalanche speeds meet in this tiny city, where they butt heads, brush shoulders, pass each other in vigilant silence.

More than any other place on earth, Jerusalem is an idea. But, paradoxically, the idea of this city is that it is possible for idea to meet action, for heaven to touch earth. In Jerusalem, there is no distance between precept and practice, between the belief and the prayer. Jerusalem is the place where concept meets concrete, where dogma meets dirt.

Time itself doesn't seem to exist there. The city's ancient underpinnings, modern realities and future speculations exist simultaneously, so that you're not quite sure if you are living in the past, present or future. When you walk through the streets of Jerusalem, you feel as though you are skirting the edge of something, performing a balancing act atop the very seam that holds together time and space.

The land of Israel seems to be at once otherworldly, and at the same time, to contain the essence and entirety of the world we know. It is the microcosm in which all the political realities, spiritual philosophies and human machinations we have discussed in this book coexist, and ultimately, the place in which they will not coexist. All roads lead to Jerusalem. Should it surprise us that it is predicted to be the site of the biggest ideological train wreck of all time?

Despite being a highly symbolic place (and despite what you may have been taught in Sunday school), Jerusalem is not a metaphor. It is not a figure of speech. Jerusalem is very real. It has school systems; it has shopping centers; it has traffic. People living in Jerusalem and throughout the land of Israel have bad days. They lock themselves out; they miss the bus. Jerusalem is the holy city in the land God calls His own. It has eternal significance and temporal importance in the redemptive story God is unfolding throughout the ages through the Jewish people—and those grafted into the tree of this faith (see Romans 11:17–18). Do we honestly think God wouldn't have a plan that encompasses every last pebble and stone of this remarkable, set-apart place?

What about this pledge made by our spiritual forebears in millennia past?

> If I forget you, O Jerusalem,
> Let my right hand forget its skill!

If I do not remember you,
Let my tongue cling to the roof of my mouth—
If I do not exalt Jerusalem
Above my chief joy.

Psalm 137:5–6

Or these words from our Savior, who wept over His people?

"O Jerusalem, Jerusalem . . . How often I wanted to gather your children together, as a hen gathers her chicks under her wings."

Matthew 23:37

See, we have made Christianity into something abstract. Ethereal. Theoretical. Much of the Church has fallen into the error of Replacement Theology—the belief that the Church completely replaces Israel. The idea that God (who created the world and went to the trouble of coming up with a plan of redemption to save it) would not uphold His connection with the land and people of Israel is preposterous. You may be called to China. You may be burdened to reach those in the business world of the West. But I have news for you: Your "Jerusalem" *is* Jerusalem!

What if your destiny, my destiny, the fate of the whole world is tied up with the outcome to be determined over this one city, this one tiny strip of desert land the size of New Jersey? Would you go there? Would you pray for this place? Would you care to make sure that, whatever your politics and persuasions are, they do not contradict what God says about Israel? Your heart should be irrevocably tied to its streets, hills, valleys and citizens. Does your heart break for Jerusalem? God's does.

Could it really be a coincidence that the Jewish people, dispersed for centuries to the four corners of the earth, should, out of the ashes of the Holocaust, be reunited with their ancient, ancestral homeland? Could it be merely chance? Good fortune? Dumb luck? No. In fact, the rebirth of the nation of Israel (God's

211

prophetic timepiece) is the number-one indicator of the times we are living in. And Jerusalem is the dividing line that God will ultimately use to measure the nations of the earth.

Have you asked yourself why there is this relentless agenda to dominate Jerusalem's airwaves, to possess its soil, to name its streets? If you haven't, you need to. We ought to be those with eyes to see and ears to hear the spiritual realities that surround us.

> **Jerusalem is the dividing line that God will ultimately use to measure the nations of the earth.**

Among the genealogical records of the tribes of Israel, we are given a powerful word in 1 Chronicles 12 about the sons of Issachar, who, as Scripture tells us, "had understanding of the times, to know what Israel ought to do" (v. 32). They were those who understood the times, demonstrating a prophetic sensitivity to what was happening in that period of history, and a sensitivity to the voice of God in the midst of it. Not only that, but they were also leaders of apostolic wisdom, those who knew how to marry the prophetic word with the proper apostolic structure to carry it out. This ancient tribe should be descriptive of the Church today, for the Church (founded on the cornerstone of Jesus Christ) is to be built upon the foundation of the apostles and the prophets (see Ephesians 2:20).

If we expect to bear fruit in the Kingdom of God, our faith needs to be rooted in the place it came from. God is jealous for Zion (see Zechariah 8:2). If we claim to have the Father's heart, we need to care about her just as much. If reading this book inspires you to do nothing else but pray for the peace of Jerusalem (according to our biblical mandate in Psalm 122:6), I will consider my mission accomplished. If you have gained nothing else from me, hear this: Jesus is returning to a people; He is returning to a place; He is returning to Jerusalem.

The Last Word

As we lay to rest the myth of coexistence, I urge us to take up the reality of shalom.

We have discovered that human conflicts are more than meets the eye, and they cannot be solved through human means. Because of this, it would be futile to look for solutions to global issues that do not take into account the ideological framework behind them. We need much more than *peace*. We need *shalom*.

The biblical word *shalom* stands for more than the absence of strife. It implies the presence of something else. It is not simply the absence of conflict that God is after; it is the full manifestation of all that is good, right, true and holy that He desires to see established. Shalom is not something that can be worked toward. It is something that is given—that appears—once all else has ceased.

By refuting the myth of coexistence and embracing the reality of shalom, we can become agents of change in the war zone of the earth. I invite you to join the remnant of resistance against the spirit of this age, and see His Kingdom come.

Notes

Introduction: "No, We Can't What?"

1. William Ury, *The Power of a Positive No: How to Say No and Still Get to Yes* (New York: Bantam Dell, 2007), 4.

2. http://www.imdb.com/title/tt0120737/quotes, "Memorable quotes for 'The Lord of the Rings: The Fellowship of the Ring,'" 2011, Internet Movie Database.

Chapter 1. What the World Needs Now

1. C. S. Lewis, *The Great Divorce* (New York: HarperCollins, 2001), VII–VIII.

Chapter 2. The End of the World As We Know It

1. John Seach, "Tambora Volcano," Volcano Live, 2010, http://www.volcano live.com/tambora.html.

2. http://en.wikipedia.org/wiki/Year_Without_a_Summer, "Year Without a Summer," March 28, 2010, Wikipedia.

3. Alexander Bell, "World at War over Water," *New Statesman*, March 28, 2010, http://www.newstatesman.com/environment/2010/03/water-cyprus-pakistan -yemen.

4. U.S. Department of State Bureau of Public Affairs, "U.S. Water Policy: Water Security Is Human Security," March 18, 2011, http://www.state.gov/r/pa/ plrmo/158737.htm.

5. Food and Agriculture Organization of the United Nations, "Global Hunger Declining, but Still Unacceptably High," Economic and Social Development Department, September 2010, http://www.fao.org/docrep/012/al390e/al390e00.pdf.

6. John von Heyking, "Iran's President and the Politics of the Twelfth Imam," Ashbrook Center for Public Affairs at Ashland University, November 2005, http://www.ashbrook.org/publicat/guest/05/vonheyking/twelfthimam.html.

7. Al Gore, *An Inconvenient Truth: The Planetary Emergency of Global Warming and What We Can Do About It* (New York: Rodale, 2006), 29.

8. Ibid, 77.

9. John Hagee, *Can America Survive? 10 Prophetic Signs That We Are the Terminal Generation* (New York: Howard Books, 2010), 7.

10. Dan Calladine, "Digital Stats," March 30, 2010, http://digital-stats.blogspot.com/2010/03/us-video-viewing-via-tv-internet-and.html.

11. http://www.onlineeducation.net/videogame, "Video Game Statistics," 2011, Education Database Online.

12. http://www.the-numbers.com/market, "US Movie Market Summary 1995 to 2011," The Numbers.

13. http://highest-grossing-movies.findthebest.com/question/31/763/How-much -money-did-2012-gross, 2011, Find the Best.

Chapter 3. Cultural Kingdoms

1. http://www.merriam-webster.com/dictionary/culture, "Culture," 2011, Merriam-Webster.

2. Ryan Dobson, *Be Intolerant: Because Some Things Are Just Stupid* (Portland: Multnomah, 2003), cover.

Chapter 4. The Three Houses

1. Samuel P. Huntington, *The Clash of Civilizations and the Remaking of World Order* (New York: Simon & Schuster, 1996), 29.

2. Adolf Hitler, *Mein Kampf*, Chapter 1, http://gutenberg.net.au/ebooks 02/0200601.txt, September 2002, Project Gutenberg Australia.

3. http://www.roman-empire.net/maps/empire/extent/rome-modern-day -nations.html, "Which modern day countries did the Roman Empire comprise of," July 3, 2009, Illustrated History of the Roman Empire.

4. Pope Paul VI, "Declaration on the Relation of the Church to Non-Christian Religions: *Nostra Aetate*," Vatican: the Holy See, October 28, 1965, http://www.vatican.va/archive/hist_councils/ii_vatican_council/documents/vat-ii_decl _19651028_nostra-aetate_en.html.

5. Islamic Resistance Movement (Hamas), "Hamas Charter," The Jerusalem Fund, 1988, http://www.thejerusalemfund.org/www.thejerusalemfund.org/carryover/documents/charter.html.

6. http://www.adherents.com/Religions_By_Adherents.html, "Major Religions of the World Ranked by Number of Adherents," August 9, 2007, adherents.com.

7. B.A. Robinson, "Religions of the World: Numbers of adherents; names of houses of worship; names of leaders; rates of growth . . . ," Ontario Consultants on Religious Tolerance, December 20, 2009, http://www.religioustolerance.org/worldrel.htm.

8. Huntington, *The Clash of Civilizations*, 175.

9. http://www.adherents.com/Religions_By_Adherents.html.

10. "YWCA loses Christianity from title," *The Telegraph,* January 7, 2011, http://www.telegraph.co.uk/news/religion/8245247/YWCA-loses-Christianity-from -title.html.

Chapter 5. The Myth of Coexistence

1. Daniel C. Juster, "Religious Coercion and Liberty of Conscience," *Israel's Restoration* 20, no. 2 (February 2011): 1.

2. Ibid, 2.

3. Ibid.

4. Douglas Harper, "tolerance," *Online Etymology Dictionary,* 2010, http://www.etymonline.com/index.php?term-tolerance.

5. Mike Emanuel and The Associated Press, "Franklin Graham Regrets Army's Decision to Rescind Invite to Pentagon Prayer Service," FOXNews .com, April 22, 2010, http://www.foxnews.com/politics/2010/04/21/army-weighs -rescinding-invitation-evangelist/#.

6. "CAIR celebrates Pentagon's disinvite of Franklin Graham," WorldNetDaily, April 23, 2010, http://www.wnd.com/?pageId=144905.

7. Greg Toppo, "ACLU sues school district to stop graduation at Conn. Church," *USA Today,* May 5, 2010, http://www.usatoday.com/news/education/2010-05-05 -church-commencement-aclu_N.htm.

8. Elliot Spagat and The Associated Press, "Judges rule cross at Calif. park unconstitutional," FOXNews.com, January 4, 2011, http://www.foxnews.com/ us/2011/01/04/judges-rule-cross-calif-park-unconstitutional/#.

9. Jonathon M. Seidl, "Calif. School Orders Boy to Remove American Flag From Bike," *TheBlaze,* November 12, 2010, http://www.theblaze.com/stories/ calif-school-orders-boy-to-remove-american-flag-from-bike.

10. Joshua Rhett Miller, "Wisconsin Veteran Must Remove Flag After Memo- rial Day, Wife Says," FOXNews.com, May 26, 2010, http://www.foxnews.com/ us/2010/05/26/wisconsin-veteran-remove-flag-memorial-day-wife-says/#.

11. "Texas Woman Told to Remove 'Offensive' American Flag From Office," FOXNews.com, May 29, 2009, http://www.foxnews.com/story/0,2933,522659,00 .html.

12. Jessica Reed, "Christianity in France is fading," guardian.co.uk, Octo- ber 14, 2010, http://www.guardian.co.uk/commentisfree/belief/2010/oct/14/ christianity-france-fading.

13. Carlos Antonio Palad, "The Collapse of the Church in France," *Rorate Caeli,* January 11, 2010, http://rorate-caeli.blogspot.com/2010/01/collapse-of -church-in-france.html.

14. http://en.wikipedia.org/wiki/Religion_in_France, "Religion in France," March 21, 2011, Wikipedia.

15. "Religion Important for Americans, Italians," *Angus Reid Global Monitor,* December 30, 2006, http://www.angus-reid.com/polls/5692/religion_important _for_americans_italians.

16. "French teacher suspended over Shoah lessons," *JTA,* September 1, 2010, http://jta.org/news/article/2010/09/01/2740745/french-teacher-suspended -over-shoah-lessons.

17. "Palestinian Maps Omitting Israel," Jewish Virtual Library, 2011, http://www.jewishvirtuallibrary.org/jsource/History/palmatoc1.html.

18. Maggie Michael, "Radical Yemeni cleric calls for killing Americans," *Washington Times*, November 8, 2010, http://www.washingtontimes.com/news/2010/nov/8/radical-yemeni-cleric-calls-killing-americans.

19. Khaled Abu Toameh, "Northern blaze delights many in the Arab world," *Jerusalem Post*, December 5, 2010, http://www.jpost.com/MiddleEast/Article.aspx?id=198002.

20. "Benjamin Franklin Requests Prayer in the Constitutional Convention," Constitution Society, 2011, http://www.constitution.org/primarysources/franklin.html.

21. *Inaugural Addresses of the Presidents of the United States: From George Washington to George W. Bush* (Washington, D.C.: U.S. G.P.O., 1989).

22. C. S. Lewis, *The Great Divorce* (New York: HarperCollins, 2001), VIII.

Chapter 6. The House of Radical Islam

1. Stuart Robinson, *Mosques and Miracles: Revealing Islam and God's Grace* (Queensland, Australia: CityHarvest Publications, 2003), 129.

2. http://www.bbc.co.uk/religion/religions/islam/holydays/alhijra.shtml, "Al-Hijra," July 9, 2009, BBC: Religions.

3. Robinson, *Mosques and Miracles*, 5.

4. Michael Scheuer, *Through Our Enemies' Eyes: Osama bin Laden, Radical Islam, and the Future of America* (Washington, D.C.: Potomac Books, 2006), 32.

5. Nonie Darwish, *Cruel and Usual Punishment: The Terrifying Global Implications of Islamic Law* (Nashville: Thomas Nelson, 2008), 197.

6. Frank Gaffney, Jr., "The Muslim Brotherhood: the enemy in its own words," Center for Security Policy, 2010, http://www.centerforsecuritypolicy.org/p18634.xml.

7. Ryan Mauro, "Muslim Enclaves U.S.A.," FrontPageMagazine, July 9, 2010, http://frontpagemag.com/2010/07/09/munslim-enclaves-u-s-a.

8. United Nations Population Fund, "Chapter 3: Ending Violence against Women and Girls," *State of World Population 2000*, 2000, http://www.unfpa.org/swp/2000/english/ch03.html.

9. Ibid.

10. J. Halaby, "Two Women, One Girl Slain in Honor Crimes in Jordan," United Nations Population Fund, March 20, 2000, http://www.unfpa.org/swp/2000/english/boxes/box20.html.

11. The Associated Press, "Iraqi 'Honor Killing' Case Begins in Arizona," CBS News, January 24, 2011, http://www.cbsnews.com/stories/2011/01/24/national/main7279009.shtml.

12. http://www.cnn.com/2008/CRIME/07/08/honor.killing/index.html, "Dad charged with murdering reluctant bride," July 9, 2008, CNN.

13. Robert Spencer, "Honor Killing in Texas," Jihad Watch, January 8, 2008, http://www.humanevents.com/article.php?id=24329#.

14. Fred O. Williams, "Possibility of 'honor killing' mulled in Orchard Park slaying," BuffaloNews.com, January 11, 2011, http://www.buffalonews.com/topics/mo-hassan/article34273.ece.

15. Robinson, *Mosques and Miracles*, 192.

16. Ibid.

17. Ibid, 193.

18. Ibid, 195.

19. Ibid, 197–198.

20. Aaron Klein, "Palestinian TV: Jews torture in name of God," *WorldNet-Daily.com*, April 4, 2005, http://www.wnd.com/index.php?fa=PAGE.printable &pageId=29668.

21. Jamie Glazov, "The Study of Political Islam," *FrontPageMagazine.com*, February 5, 2007, http://archive.frontpagemag.com/readArticle.aspx?ARTID=297#.

22. "Arafat in Stockholm," Arutz-7, February 27, 1996, http://www.professors .org.il/docs/stock.htm.

Chapter 7. The House of Militant Secularism

1. Richard Dawkins, *The God Delusion* (New York: Houghton Mifflin, 2008), 51.

2. John Dewey, *A Common Faith (The Terry Lecture Series)* (New Haven: Yale University Press, 1934), cover.

3. Charles Francis Potter, *Humanism: A New Religion* (New York: Simon and Schuster, 1930), 128.

4. http://www.christian.org.uk/news/video-mall-blocks-christmas-song-to -avoid-religious-bias, "Video: Mall blocks Christmas song to avoid 'religious bias,'" December 22, 2010, The Christian Institute.

5. Associated Press, "University of Illinois Instructor Fired Over Catholic Beliefs," FOXNews.com, July 9, 2010, http://www.foxnews.com/us/2010/07/09/ university-illinois-instructor-fired-catholic-beliefs.

6. James Perloff, "Holodomor: The Secret Holocaust in Ukraine," The Security Service of Ukraine, February 11, 2009, http://www.sbu.gov.ua/sbu/control/en/ publish/article?art_id=84758&cat_id=83648.

7. William Harms, "China's Great Leap Forward," *The University of Chicago Chronicle* 15, no. 13 (March 14, 1996) http://chronicle.uchicago.edu/960314/china .shtml.

8. David Thomas, Ph. D, "Winning Teams: Karl Marx—1818–1883 AD," 2011, http://winning-teams.com/philosophy/marx.html.

9. Karl Marx, poem "The Pale Maiden," quoted in Richard Wurmbrand, *Was Karl Marx a Satanist?* (Unknown Binding), 20.

10. Karl Marx, Untitled poem, quoted in Wurmbrand, *Was Karl Marx a Satanist?* 7.

11. Karl Marx, drama *Oulanem,* quoted in Wurmbrand, *Was Karl Marx a Satanist?* 12.

12. Letter to Marx, March 2, 1837, quoted in Wurmbrand, *Was Karl Marx a Satanist?* 16.

13. http://www.imdb.com/title/tt0038650/quotes, "Memorable quotes for 'It's a Wonderful Life,'" 2011, Internet Movie Database.

Chapter 8. The House of Judeo-Christianity

1. Francis A. Schaeffer, *How Should We Then Live?* (New Jersey: Fleming H. Revell, 1976).

2. Thomas Cahill, *The Gifts of the Jews: How a Tribe of Desert Nomads Changed the Way Everyone Thinks and Feels* (New York: Anchor Books, 1998), 93–94.
3. C. S. Lewis, *Mere Christianity* (New York: Simon & Schuster, 1996).
4. http://www.archives.gov/exhibits/charters/declaration_transcript.html, "The Declaration of Independence: A Transcription," 2011, U.S. National Archives and Records Administration.
5. http://www.mccl.org/Page.aspx?pid=400, "United States Abortion Statistics," 2010, Minnesota Citizens Concerned for Life.

Chapter 9. The Spirituality of the Three Houses

1. Josh Loposer, "Majority of Americans Believe Pets Have Psychic Powers," pawnation, January 12, 2011, http://www.pawnation.com/2011/01/12/majority -of-americans-believe-pets-have-psychic-powers.
2. Debbie Ford, "Consciousness Cleanse Day 3: The Gift of Release," Oprah. com, January 5, 2010, http://www.oprah.com/spirit/Consciousness-Cleanse -Day-3-The-Gift-of-Release.
3. "Living the Law of Attraction," *The Oprah Winfrey Show*, June 27, 2008, http://www.oprah.com/spirit/The-Law-of-Attraction-Real-Life-Stories_1.
4. Ed and Deb Shapiro, "How Meditation Can Save Your Relationship," Oprah.com, April 16, 2010, http://www.oprah.com/spirit/How-Meditation-Can -Save-Your-Relationship.
5. Curtis M. Wong, "Muslims Mark Day Of Ashura With Self-Flagellation Rituals (PHOTOS)," HuffPost World, March 23, 2011, http://www.huffingtonpost. com/2010/12/17/ashura-muslim-holiday_n_798206.html#s210456.
6. http://www.wnd.com/?pageId=34177, "Trouble in the Holy Land: Palestinian candidate mother of 'martyrs,'" January 4, 2006, *WorldNetDaily*.
7. Mitchell D. Silber and Arvin Bhatt, *Radicalization in the West: the Home-grown Threat,* New York Police Department Intelligence Division, 2007, http:// www.investigativeproject.org/documents/testimony/344.pdf, 25–26.
8. Walt Hunter, Tony Hanson, and John Ostapkovich, "Philadelphia Abortion Doctor Charged With 8 Counts Of Murder," CBSPhilly.com, January 19, 2011, http://philadelphia.cbslocal.com/2011/01/19/philly-doctor-facing-8-counts -of-murder.
9. Carolyn C. Gargaro, "Quotes About Abortion," In Memory of Mother Teresa page, 2002, http://www.gargaro.com/mother_teresa/quotes.html.
10. Nathan Pitchford, "The Blood of the Martyrs," Reformation Theology, May 21, 2006, http://www.reformationtheology.com/2006/05/the_blood_of_the _martyrs.php.

Chapter 10. Will the Real World Please Stand Up?

1. Mitchell D. Silber and Arvin Bhatt, *Radicalization in the West: the Home-grown Threat,* New York Police Department Intelligence Division, 2007, http:// www.investigativeproject.org/documents/testimony/344.pdf, 25–26.
2. Aatish Taseer, "The killer of my father, Salman Taseer, was showered with rose petals by fanatics. How could they do this?" *The Telegraph*, January 8, 2011,

http://www.telegraph.co.uk/news/worldnews/asia/pakistan/8248162/The-killer
-of-my-father-Salman-Taseer-was-showered-with-rose-petals-by-fanatics.-How
-could-they-do-this.html.

3. http://www.dailymail.co.uk/news/article-1354246/One-legged-Afghan
-Red-Cross-worker-hanged-converting-Christianity.html, "One-legged Afghan
Red Cross worker set to be hanged after converting to Christianity," February 7,
2011, *Mail Online*.

4. Patrick Goodenough, "UAE Official Tries to Explain Court Ruling Upholding Muslim Men's Right to Beat Their Wives," CNSNews.com, October 21, 2010,
http://www.cnsnews.com/news/article/uae-official-tries-explain-court-ruling#.

5. http://www.emirates247.com/news/region/women-with-seditious-eyes-must
-cover-up-2010-11-14-1.317325, "Women with 'seditious' eyes must cover up,"
November 14, 2010, *Emirates 24/7 News*.

6. Elad Benari, "Austria: Judge Rules That Yodeling Offends Muslims," Arutz
Sheva, December 15, 2010, http://www.israelnationalnews.com/News/News.aspx
/141152.

7. Mike Shedlock, "Beware The Ice Age Cometh: Hackers Prove Global Warming Is A Scam," Mish's Global Economic Trend Analysis, November 21, 2009, http://
globaleconomicanalysis.blogspot.com/2009/11/hackers-prove-global-warming
-is-scam.html.

8. *30 Rock*: Season 4, Episode 6, "Sun Tea," aired November 19, 2009.

9. Clyde F. Autio, "What is your worldview?" Answers in Genesis, May 2, 2005,
http://www.answersingenesis.org/docs2005/0502worldview.asp#n1.

10. Barry A. Kosmin and Ariela Keysar, *American Religious Identification
Survey (ARIS 2008)*, March 2009, http://www.americanreligionsurvey-aris.org/
reports/ARIS_Report_2008.pdf, 3.

11. Jennifer Riley, "Survey: Less Than 1 Percent of Young Adults Hold Biblical Worldview," Christian Post, March 10, 2009, http://www.christianpost.com/
news/survey-less-than-1-percent-of-young-adults-hold-biblical-worldview-37415/.

12. James P. Gannon, "Is God dead in Europe?" *USA Today*, January 15, 2006,
http://www.usatoday.com/news/opinion/editorials/2006-01-08-faith-edit_x.htm.

13. http://www.christianity.com/ChurchHistory/11630859, "The Explosion of
Christianity in Africa," 2001, Christianity.com.

14. David P. Goldman (pseud. "Spengler"), "Christianity finds a fulcrum in
Asia," *Asia Times Online*, August 7, 2007, http://www.atimes.com/atimes/China/
IH07Ad03.html.

15. http://www.fas.harvard.edu/~phildept/about.html, "Harvard University:
Department of Philosophy," 2011, Harvard University website.

16. http://acheritagegroup.org/blog/?p=387, "John Hancock—Benevolent Pa-
triot," March 10, 2010, American Christian Heritage blog.

17. http://www.beliefnet.com/resourcelib/docs/21/Benjamin_Franklins
_Request_for_Prayers_at_the_Constitutional__1.html, "Benjamin Franklin's Re-
quest for Prayers at the Constitutional Convention," 2011, beliefnet Founding
Faith Archive.

18. Terry Covey, "Seeds of Faith," Today in the Word, March 31, 2009, http://
pastorterryblog.wordpress.com/2009/03/31/prophetic-words-concerning-america.

19. Soeren Kern, "The Spanish Ham Lawsuit and Other Muslim Problems Hitting Iberia," Hudson New York, December 23, 2010, http://www.hudson-ny.org/1745/spanish-muslim-ham-lawsuit.

20. David J. Rusin, "Europe Wakes to Multiculturalism's Epic Failure," Islamist Watch, February 18, 2011, http://www.islamist-watch.org/blog/2011/02/europe-wakes-to-multiculturalism-epic-failure.

21. Josh Sanburn, "People Who Mattered: Feisal Abdul Rauf, Muslim-American Leader," TIME, December 15, 2010, http://www.time.com/time/specials/packages/article/0,28804,2036683_2036767_2036812,00.html.

22. Glynnis MacNicol, "NBC Names Ground Zero Mosque Developer A 'Person of the Year,'" Business Insider, November 26, 2010, http://www.businessinsider.com/cue-outrage-nbc-names-park-51-developer-a-person-of-the-year-2010-11.

23. http://contenderministries.org/UN/globalismquotes.php, "Quotes from Globalists and International Leaders," October 15, 2002, Contender Ministries.

24. Richard Kerbaj, "Muslim population 'rising 10 times faster than rest of society,'" The Times, January 30, 2009, http://www.timesonline.co.uk/tol/news/uk/article5621482.ece.

25. Dr. Taj Hargey, "What has Britain come to when it takes a Muslim like me to defend Christianity?" Mail Online, April 8, 2010, http://www.dailymail.co.uk/debate/article-1264399/What-Britain-come-takes-Muslim-like-defend-Christianity.html.

DR. ROBERT STEARNS is the founder and executive director of Eagles' Wings, a dynamic relational ministry involved in a variety of outreaches and strategic projects around the world. He and the Eagles' Wings team are dedicated to bringing unity and awakening to the Body of Christ. He has ministered in thirty nations around the world and maintains a significant burden for the eastern United States and for Israel.

Robert is the visionary behind the worldwide prayer initiative, "The Day of Prayer for the Peace of Jerusalem," which is observed every year the first Sunday in October. Robert and Dr. Jack Hayford serve together as co-chairmen of the mass prayer mobilization, representing the largest coalition of leaders of influence in the Body of Christ focused upon prayer for Jerusalem.

Robert has consulted and met personally with current and past prime ministers of Israel Ehud Olmert, Ariel Sharon and Benjamin Netanyahu concerning Israel and Christian relations. He has also sung for the last four prime ministers, including a special concert for Benjamin Netanyahu. In Israel he has been keynote speaker, guest artist and worship leader at several celebrations of the Feast of Tabernacles and has ministered in congregations throughout the land.

A powerful communicator and musician, Robert has been a featured guest columnist in both *Charisma* and *Ministry Today* magazines, is in demand internationally as a keynote speaker, worship leader and soloist, and has lectured in colleges and universities across America. Robert is an accomplished author and recording artist. He has made numerous television appearances, including on *The 700 Club* with Pat Robertson, *100 Huntley Street, Praise the Lord* on the Trinity Broadcasting Network and on *Celebration* with Marcus and Joni Lamb on the Daystar network.

Robert serves on the board of directors of the King's University and is the publisher of *KAIROS* magazine, as well as the executive director of the Israel Experience College Scholarship Program. Robert was the executive director of "The Call New York City," which gathered 90,000 people for prayer and fasting in New York City in June 2002. In 2005 he served on the leadership committee for the New York City Billy Graham Crusade, the last of Mr. Graham's career. Robert served on the executive cabinet and as the international worship coordinator for the 2006 Azusa Centennial Celebration.

In February 2008 Robert received the Ed McAteer Tree of Life Award, recognizing his commitment and dedication to the Jewish people and the State of Israel.

Robert and his family live in New York, and spend a great deal of time in Jerusalem, Israel.

"Robert Stearns challenges us to recognize and confront forces of extremism that threaten the values of freedom and opportunity around the world."

Senator Joseph Lieberman

"Robert Stearns' proven leadership is a beacon of insight both within the Body of Christ and beyond. Robert brings balanced and informed perspective to the critical issues facing our world with clarity, competence and compassion."

Jack Hayford, founding pastor, The Church On The Way, Van Nuys, California

"The culture of the 21st century (defined by Dr. George Hunter as The New Apostolic Age) is almost identical to the culture of the first-century Church. Today is truly the age of the 'clash of cultures.' Concerned people are asking questions that do not have easy or simplistic answers. Robert Stearns, in his profound new book, *No, We Can't*, gives us an assessment of the vital issues the Church faces in this complex and diverse world. It is a book born to be read by every thinking person attempting to find his or her way in this unbelievably complex world."

Tommy Reid, founding senior pastor, The Tabernacle, Buffalo, New York

"Robert Stearns presents provocative approaches to some of life's difficult dilemmas, and to the deeper questions of meaning that touch us in the modern world."

David Wolpe, rabbi, Sinai Temple, Los Angeles, California

"Robert Stearns does for us in this book what the very best real estate agents do for us when we seek to find a home. He walks us through the neighborhood of worldview thinking, lets us enter the houses and look around and then honestly points out the differences. But this book is not about real estate—it is about life and eternity. Robert chooses the hard road of stating his mind and convictions based on a biblical worldview. Sometimes that is difficult, but after reading what Robert has to say, I am grateful we have his voice."

Jerry Gillis, lead pastor, The Chapel at CrossPoint, Getzville, New York

"This book is such a timely, awakening word for Christians to understand the three primary worldviews that are prevalent today and how we must respond by God's leading. We cannot ignore what is in opposition to our Christian faith and hope it will just go away. The love of Christ compels us to reach this world, and I believe you will be inspired as you read *No, We Can't* to live, to demonstrate and to speak to others the Gospel of Jesus Christ."

Sharon Daugherty, pastor, Victory Christian Center, Tulsa, Oklahoma